UNDERSTANDING
JOHN GUARE

UNDERSTANDING CONTEMPORARY AMERICAN LITERATURE

Matthew J. Bruccoli, Founding Editor

Linda Wagner-Martin, Series Editor

UNDERSTANDING
JOHN GUARE

William W. Demastes

The University of South Carolina Press

Published by the University of South Carolina Press
Columbia, South Carolina 29208

www.sc.edu/uscpress

Manufactured in the United States of America

26 25 24 23 22 21 20 19 18 17
10 9 8 7 6 5 4 3 2 1

Library of Congress Cataloging-in-Publication Data

Names: Demastes, William W., author.
Title: Understanding John Guare / William W. Demastes.
Description: Columbia : The University of South Carolina Press, 2017. | Series: Understanding contemporary American literature | Includes bibliographical references and index.
Identifiers: LCCN 2016054277 (print) | LCCN 2016054680 (ebook) | ISBN 9781611177381 (hardback) | ISBN 9781611177398 (ebook)
Subjects: LCSH: Guare, John. | BISAC: LITERARY CRITICISM / American / General. | PERFORMING ARTS / Theater / Playwriting.
Classification: LCC PS3557.U2 Z57 2017 (print) | LCC PS3557.U2 (ebook) | DDC 812/.54 [B]—dc23
LC record available at https://lccn.loc.gov/2016054277

This book was printed on recycled paper with
30 percent postconsumer waste content.

CONTENTS

SERIES EDITOR'S PREFACE

The Understanding Contemporary American Literature series was founded by the estimable Matthew J. Bruccoli (1931–2008), who envisioned these volumes as guides or companions for students as well as good nonacademic readers, a legacy that will continue as new volumes are developed to fill in gaps among the nearly one hundred series volumes published to date and to embrace a host of new writers only now making their marks on our literature.

As Professor Bruccoli explained in his preface to the volumes he edited, because much influential contemporary literature makes special demands, "the word understanding in the titles was chosen deliberately. Many willing readers lack an adequate understanding of how contemporary literature works; that is, of what the author is attempting to express and the means by which it is conveyed." Aimed at fostering this understanding of good literature and good writers, the criticism and analysis in the series provide instruction in how to read certain contemporary writers—explicating their material, language, structures, themes, and perspectives—and facilitate a more profitable experience of the works under discussion.

In the twenty-first century Professor Bruccoli's prescience gives us an avenue to publish expert critiques of significant contemporary American writing. The series continues to map the literary landscape and to provide both instruction and enjoyment. Future volumes will seek to introduce new voices alongside canonized favorites, to chronicle the changing literature of our times, and to remain, as Professor Bruccoli conceived, contemporary in the best sense of the word.

Linda Wagner-Martin, Series Editor

ACKNOWLEDGMENTS

All thanks go to John Guare himself. He chose not to call security when an enthusiastic theatergoer jumped onstage to introduce himself. Later Guare agreed to share information and insights with this same theatergoer when the idea of a book came up. Reading Guare's work over the years should have prepared me for the fact that nothing would really surprise Mr. Guare, including a stalking academic. Thanks, John.

Thanks also go to ever-patient Jean and Erin, who help in these projects in numerous ways, tangible and otherwise.

PROFESSIONAL CHRONOLOGY

Performances and Readings

1966

Something I'll Tell You Tuesday and *The Loveliest Afternoon of the Year* are presented by Joe Cino at the Caffe Cino, New York City, 25 October, directed by Russ Kaiser.

1967

A Day for Surprises is presented by Joe Cino at the Caffe Cino, New York City, August, directed by Bernie Wagner.

Muzeeka is first performed at the Eugene O'Neill Memorial Theatre, Waterford, Conn., 19 July, directed by Melvin Bernhardt. It is also performed at the Mark Taper Forum in the Los Angeles Music Center, 10 October, directed by Edward Parone. The cast includes Philip Proctor, Sheree North, and Philip Austin.

1968

Muzeeka opens at the Provincetown Playhouse, New York City, 28 April, directed by Melvin Bernhardt, starring Sam Waterston, Marcia Jean Kurtz, and Peggy Pope. A Waterford Company Production. It wins an Obie Award.

Cop-Out is performed at the Eugene O'Neill Theater Center, Waterford, Conn., July, directed by Melvin Benhardt, starring Ron Leibman and Linda Lavin.

1969

Cop-Out is produced at Cort Theatre, New York, April, directed by Melvin Bernhardt, starring Ron Leibman and Linda Lavin.

Home Fires is performed as curtain-raiser for Cort Theatre production of *Cop-Out*.

Kissing Sweet, a one-act television play, airs 25 November on the New York Television Theater as part of a commissioned series of plays about pollution, *FOUL!*

1971

The House of Blue Leaves premieres at the Truck and Warehouse Theatre, New York, 10 February, directed by Mel Shapiro, presented by Warren Lyons and Betty Ann Besch. It wins the New York Drama Critics' Circle Award for best American play.

Two Gentlemen of Verona, a musical adaptation by John Guare and Mel Shapiro, opens at the New York Shakespeare Festival, Central Park. Lyrics by Guare, music by Galt MacDermot. Cast includes Frank O'Brien, Alix Elias, Clifton Davis, Alvin Lum, Rául Juliá, Jerry Stiller, Carla Pinza, and Norman Matlock. It opens 1 December at the St. James Theatre, New York, winning the 1972 New York Drama Critics' Circle Award for best musical and Tony Awards for best musical and best book. Guare receives the Drama Desk Award for outstanding lyrics.

Taking Off (film), cowritten by Guare, Milos Forman, Jean-Claude Carrière, and John Klein, is released. Directed by Forman.

1973

Two Gentlemen of Verona receives a London West End production at the Phoenix Theatre, opening 26 April and running for 237 performances.

Marco Polo Sings a Solo opens July at the Nantucket Stage Company, Mass., directed by Mel Shapiro and featuring Piper Laurie, Beeson Carroll, and Kevin O'Connor.

1974

Rich and Famous is produced in August by William Gardner at the Academy Festival Theater, Lake Forest, Ill., directed by Mel Shapiro, starring Ron Leibman, Linda Lavin, Charles Kimbrough, and William Jay. It transfers to Williamstown (Mass.) Theater Festival same month.

1976

Rich and Famous is produced by the New York Shakespeare Festival, 19 February, directed by Mel Shapiro, featuring Ron Leibman, Anita Gillette, and William Atherton. Music and lyrics by Guare.

1977

Landscape of the Body is produced in July by William Gardner at the Academy Festival Theatre, Lake Forest, Ill., directed by John Pasquin, starring Shirley Knight, F. Murray Abraham, and Peg Murray. Settings by John Wulp, lighting by Jennifer Tipton. It transfers to the Public Theatre, New York City, 12 October, presented by Joseph Papp and the New York Shakespeare Festival, settings by Santo Loquasto.

Marco Polo Sings a Solo presented by the New York Shakespeare Festival, produced by Joseph Papp, opens 6 February at New York's Public Theatre. Directed by Mel Shapiro, starring Madeline Kahn, Chris Sarandon, Sigourney Weaver, and Joel Grey. Setting by John Wulp, lighting by Jennifer Tipton.

1979

Bosoms and Neglect opens 3 May at the Longacre Theatre, New York City, following an initial engagement at the Goodman Theatre, Chicago (Gregory Mosher, artistic director), that opened 1 March. The cast includes Kate Reid, Paul Rudd, and Marian Mercer. Directed by Mel Shapiro, presented by Bernard Gersten and John Wulp. Scenery by John Wulp, lighting by Jennifer Tipton.

1980

Atlantic City (film), screenplay by Guare, is released. Directed by Louis Malle, starring Susan Sarandon, Burt Lancaster, and Kate Reid. Wins the Golden Lion Award for best film at the Venice Film Festival. It is nominated for five Academy Awards, including best original screenplay.

1981

In Fireworks Lie Secret Codes is presented by Lincoln Center Theater, New York City, at the Mitzi E. Newhouse Theater, 5 March, as part of the Lincoln Center One Act Play Festival. Directed by Guare, starring William Newman, Kathleen Widdoes, and James Woods.

1982

Lydie Breeze opens 25 February at the American Place Theater, New York City, presented and scenery by John Wulp, directed by Louis Malle, starring Cynthia Nixon, Roberta Maxwell, and Madeleine Potter.

Gardenia opens 28 April at the Manhattan Theater Club, New York City, directed by Karel Reisz, starring Sam Waterston, JoBeth Williams, Edward Herrmann, and James Woods. Design by Santo Loquasto, lighting by Craig Miller, costumes by Ann Roth.

1984

Women and Water, first draft, is produced at the Los Angeles Actors Theater, directed by Bill Bushnell and starring Laurie O'Brien and David Huffman.

1985

Women and Water is presented in November at the Arena Stage, Washington, D.C., a Zelda Finchlander production, directed by Doug Wager, starring Cary Anne Spear, John Leonard, and Casey Biggs.

The Talking Dog, a short play commissioned as part of *Orchards*—a collection inspired by the short stories of Anton Chekhov—is presented by the Acting Company (John Houseman, artistic director), which toured the United States with these plays, 1985–86. Other contributors include Maria Irene Fornés, Spalding Gray, David Mamet, Wendy Wasserstein, Michael Weller, and Samm-Art Williams. Directed by Robert Falls.

1986

The House of Blue Leaves is revived 19 March at the Mitzi Newhouse Theater of Lincoln Center, New York City. Directed by Jerry Zaks, starring John Mahoney, Ben Stiller, Stockard Channing, Swoosie Kurtz, Julie Hagerty, and Christopher Walken. With notable cast changes, the production transfers to Lincoln Center's Vivian Beaumont Theater and to the Plymouth Theater, New York City, on 14 October. The production wins four Tony Awards.

Two Gentlemen of Verona is produced by the New Jersey Shakespeare Festival. Directed by Robert Duke, starring Philip Hernandez and Dana M. Reeve.

Bosoms and Neglect, directed by Larry Arrick, starring Anne Meara, is revived at the Perry Street Theatre, New York City, April, produced by the New York Theater Workshop.

1987

Moon under Miami (originally *Moon over Miami*) is first produced in August at the Williamstown (Mass.) Theatre Festival, directed by Larry Sloan and featuring Nathan Lane, Julie Hagerty, Glenne Headly, and James Belushi.

The Race to Urga, a musical based on Bertolt Brecht's play *The Exception and the Rule,* begun in 1968 but never mounted, is given a workshop production, April–May, at the Mitzi Newhouse Theater at Lincoln Center, New York City. Directed and choreographed by Jerome Robbins. Music by Leonard Bernstein.

Lincoln Center Theater Review is founded by John Guare. It is coedited (to present) with Anne Cataneo.

1988

Women and Water is recorded in June by BBC Radio, directed by Stuart Owen, starring Natasha Richardson, Trevor Eve, and Frank Grimes. During the summer, an Atlantic Theater Company production (summer) is performed in Montpelier, Vt. Directed by Stephen Schacter, starring Mary McCann, Todd Weeks, and Jordan Lage.

1989

Moon over Miami is produced by Yale Repertory Theatre, New Haven, Conn., in April. Directed by Andrei Belgrader, starring Oliver Platt, Tony Shalhoub, and Julie Hagerty.

1990

Six Degrees of Separation premieres 19 May at the Mitzi E. Newhouse Theater, Lincoln Center Theater, New York City, presented by Gregory Mosher and Bernard Gersten. Directed by Jerry Zaks, starring Stockard Channing, John Cunningham, Sam Stoneburner, and James McDaniel. Sets by Tony Walton, lighting by Paul Gallo. Kelly Bishop and then Swoosie Kurtz replace Channing, 1 August–28 October. Channing returns 8 November when the production moves to the Vivian Beaumont Theatre, Lincoln Center, New York City, with Courtney B. Vance playing Paul. It wins an Obie Award, the New York Drama Critics' Circle Award, and London's Olivier Award for best play and is a finalist for the Pulitzer Prize in drama.

1992

Four Baboons Adoring the Sun is produced by Lincoln Center Theater at the Vivian Beaumont Theater, New York City, 18 March. Music by Stephen Edwards, set by Tony Walton. Directed by Sir Peter Hall, starring Stockard Channing, James Naughton, and Eugene Perry. It is nominated for a Tony Award for best play.

New York Actor (one act) premieres April at a benefit for the American Repertory Theater, Cambridge, Mass., Robert Brustein, artistic director.

1993

New York Actor (expanded one act) is presented at the New York Public Library for the Performing Arts Reading Room Series, 1 February. Directed by Neel Keller, starring John Vickery, Stephen Pearlman, Jerry Stiller, Marian Seldes, and André Gregory.

Six Degrees of Separation (film) is released, directed by Fred Schepisi, starring Stockard Channing, Donald Sutherland, and Will Smith.

1994

New York Actor is further expanded for the Ensemble Theater Marathon Series, New York City, and opens 18 May. Directed by Jerry Zaks, starring Bradley Whitford.

1995

Moon under Miami is produced by Remains Theater, Chicago, April, directed by Neel Keller, scenery by Red Grooms.

Chuck Close: A Life 1988–1995, written by Guare, is published by Thames and Hudson, New York.

1998

The General of Hot Desire ("inspired by Shakespeare's Sonnets 153 and 154 and "the Golden Legend by Jacobus De Voragine [1229–1298]") premieres at the

Guthrie Theater Lab 7, Minneapolis, Minn., in January. Part of an evening titled *Love's Fire,* including seven plays inspired by seven Shakespeare sonnets, by Guare, Eric Bogosian, Ntozake Shange, Marsha Norman, Tony Kushner, William Finn, and Wendy Wasserstein. Directed by Mark Lamos, music by Adam Guettel. Tours America in a series of one-night performances, opens at the Barbican Theatre, London, 20 May, and reopens at the Joseph Papp Public Theater, New York City, 22 June.

Greenwich Mean is commissioned and produced by the American Repertory Theater, Cambridge, Mass., Robert Brustein, artistic director, for a short play festival, April.

New York Actor (final version) opens as part of the Ensemble Studio Theater, New York City, Twenty-fifth Anniversary Classics Series, 14 March. It is directed by Keith Reddin.

Marco Polo Sings a Solo, directed by Mel Shapiro, starring Bruce Norris and Polly Holliday, and *Bosoms and Neglect,* directed by Nicholas Martin, starring Katie Fineran and Mary Louise Wilson, are presented as part of a John Guare season, Signature Theater, New York City, founded by James Houghton.

1999

Lake Hollywood premieres at the Signature Theater, New York City, 29 April, James Houghton artistic director. Directed by Doug Hughes and Itamar Kubovy, starring Kate Burton and Betty Miller. Transfers to the Guthrie Theater, Minneapolis, Minn.

Chaucer in Rome opens at the Williamstown (Mass.) Theater Festival, 28 July, directed by Nicholas Martin, set by Alexander Dodge. It features B. D. Wong, Kali Rocha, and Bruce Norris.

2000

Lydie Breeze, Parts I (Bullfinch's Mythology) and II (The Sacredness of the Next Task) is presented at the New York Theatre Workshop, New York City, 15 May. Directed by Itamar Kubovy, scenery by Brian McDevitt, music by Adam Guettel. Starring Elizabeth Marvel and Bill Camp.

2001

Chaucer in Rome is produced by Lincoln Center Theater, New York City, 7 June, André Bishop, artistic director. Directed by Nicholas Martin, set design by Alexander Dodge. Starring Jon Tenney, Carrie Preston, and Bruce Norris.

2002

A Few Stout Individuals is commissioned and produced by the Signature Theatre Company, New York City, 12 May, James Houghton, artistic director.

Directed by Michael Greif, set by Allen Moyer. Starring James Yaegashi, Donald Moffat, Polly Holiday, and William Sadler.

Sweet Smell of Success, a musical adaptation of the film, book by Guare, music by Marvin Hamlisch, lyrics by Craig Cornelia, plays 5 January–2 February at the Wit Theater, Chicago. Transfers to the Martin Beck Theater, New York City, 14 March–15 June. Directed by Nicholas Hytner, starring John Lithgow, Brian d'Arcy James, and Kelli O'Hara. Guare receives a Tony nomination for best book of a musical.

2003

Woman at a Threshold, Beckoning (one act) is performed at Marathon 2003, the Twenty-Sixth Annual Festival of One-Act Plays, Series B, at the E.S.T. Theatre, New York City.

His Girl Friday, an adaptation of Ben Hecht and Charles MacArthur's play and film *The Front Page* and commissioned by Nicholas Hytner, premieres 5 June at the Royal National Theatre's Olivier Theatre, London. Starring Alex Jennings and Zoë Wanamaker.

2005

Two Gentlemen of Verona is revived by the Public Theater in its Shakespeare in the Park series, Delacorte Theater, New York City. Directed by Kathleen Marshall, starring Oscar Isaac and Norman Lewis.

Landscape of the Body is revived at the Signature Theatre Company, New York City, April–May. Directed by Michael Grief, starring Lili Taylor and Sherry Rene Scott.

U.S. production of *His Girl Friday* opens at the Guthrie Theatre, Minneapolis, Minn. in July. Directed by Joe Dowling, starring Courtney B. Vance and Angela Bassett.

2007

Blue Monologue (one act) is produced as part of a collection, *Five Story Walk-up,* Daniel Gallant producer, 21 March, at the Thirteenth Street Rep Theatre, New York City.

2009

Rich and Famous, directed by John Rando, is reworked and performed at American Conservatory Theater, San Francisco, January–February. Starring Brooks Ashmanskas, Stephen DeRosa, and Mary Birdsong.

2010

What It Was Like (monologue) is produced as part of a collection titled *Seven Card Draw,* Daniel Gallant executive producer, at Dixon Place, New York City, 16–18 March.

A Free Man of Color premieres 23 October at the Vivian Beaumont Theatre, Lincoln Center, New York City, André Bishop, artistic director. Directed by George C. Wolfe, starring Jeffrey Wright and Mos Def. Sets by David Rockwell, costumes by Anne Hould-Ward. It is a finalist for the Pulitzer Prize in drama.

2011

House of Blue Leaves opens 25 April at Walter Kerr Theater, New York City. Directed by David Cromer, starring Ben Stiller, Edie Falco, and Jennifer Jason Leigh.

Elzbieta Erased, commissioned by the Atlantic Theater Company, New York City, premieres on 18 May, at an art gallery on Vinalhaven Island, Maine. Guare plays one of the play's two roles. The play is part of Guare's forthcoming collection *3 Kinds of Exile.*

2012

Are You There, McPhee? opens 11 May at the McCarter Theatre, Princeton, N.J. Directed by Sam Buntrock, starring Paul Gross.

The Sea, a ten-minute monologue, directed by Craig Baldwin, starring Sam Tsoutsouvas, is performed at a benefit for the Red Bull Theater at St. Clement's Church on W. Forty-Sixth Street, New York City, on 18 June.

A Free Man of Color opens 21 September at the Claude L. Shaver Theatre, Baton Rouge, La., as part of Louisiana's bicentennial celebration of statehood. Directed by Paul Russell, starring Alvin Keith.

2013

3 Kinds of Exile—comprising three Guare short pieces, *Karel, Elzbieta Erased,* and *Funiage*—is staged in June at the Atlantic Theater Company, New York City. The production includes Guare in an acting role, marking his professional acting debut.

Lydie Breeze is restaged at Chicago's Greenhouse Theater Center in November.

His Girl Friday is revived at the La Jolla Playhouse, La Jolla, Calif.

2014

Between, part of an evening of short plays called *Nine Signs of the Times,* Daniel Gallant producer, plays 11–13 April, at the Nuyorican Poets Café, New York City. In June, Theater Breaking Through Boundaries produces *Between* in New York City as part of an evening called *Power Plays.* The TBTB production tours Japan in October. *Between* also performed by Stockard Channing and John Guare and directed by Jack O'Brien at NeueHouse in New York City on 3 November.

2015

His Girl Friday is produced August 6–30 at the Barrington Staged Company, Pittsfield, Mass. Directed by Julianne Boyd, starring Christopher Innvar and Jane Pfitsch.

More Stars Than There Are in Heaven, an adaptation of a Tennessee Williams short story, is given a staged reading 17 September at the Playhouse Creatures Theatre Co., New York City, in association with the Tennessee Williams Festival. Directed by Cosmin Chivu, starring Lusia Strus. Music by Natalie Tannenbaum.

You Lied to Me about Centralia, an adaptation of a Tennessee Williams short story, is produced 2 September–10 October by the Acting Company at 59 E. Fifty-Ninth Street Theater, New York City. The event, called *Desire,* also includes works by Beth Henley, Marcus Gardley, Rebecca Gilman, David Grimm, and Elizabeth Egloff.

Awards and Honors

1981

Guare receives the Award of Merit from the American Academy of Arts and Letters for his plays *The House of Blue Leaves, Rich and Famous, Marco Polo Sings a Solo, Landscape of the Body,* and *Bosoms and Neglect.*

1989

The American Academy and Institute of Arts and Letters elects Guare a member.

1993

Guare is elected to the Theatre Hall of Fame.

1996

Guare receives the New York State Governor's Arts Award.

1998–1999

The Signature Theatre, New York City, honors Guare with a season dedicated to his work.

1999

Guare is honored at the William Inge Festival, Independence, Kansas.

2003

Guare receives the PEN/Laura Pels International Foundation for Theater Award for a master American dramatist.

2004

Guare receives the Gold Medal in Drama from the American Academy of Arts and Letters.

2005

Guare receives an Obie Award for sustained excellence.

2014

Guare receives a lifetime achievement award from the Dramatists Guild.

2015

Guare receives the Erwin Piscator Award for excellence in the theater.

CHAPTER 1

Understanding John Guare

Life is the unconscious, writing the conscious.

John Guare, quoted in Henry Hewes,
"The Playwright as Voyager"

John Guare has had a long and distinguished career in the American theater. Coming to the scene during the tumultuous 1960s and active well into the second decade of the twenty-first century, Guare is very much a man of the age, equipped with a flexibility of mind and style to embrace the disruptures, disjunctures, and transformations that distinguish the decades he has experienced as some of the most destabilized and uncertain in America's history. Right and wrong, good and bad have become terms whose applications have become at best relative, at worst meaningless. Finding authenticity in a world lost in uncertainty required more than common skills and talents.

Into this world entered playwrights such as Guare and contemporaries Edward Albee, Sam Shepard, and David Mamet, who recognized that truths once held to be self-evident, even in the recent past, no longer offered the comfort and solace they once did. Not only did they not provide a shelter against the oncoming storm, these truths sometimes were actually dangerous, even life threatening, to those who refused to pause and evaluate what they held to be true and worthy. Confronting these issues with fearlessness, these writers brought what Gene A. Plunka, in his 2002 study *The Black Comedy of John Guare,* calls "renewed life to the contemporary American theater."[1] The theater of these playwrights undertook to evaluate everything and challenge sacred cows such as the American dream, the White Anglo-Saxon work ethic, and Judeo-Christian traditions in general.

Plunka observes that in the 1960s and 1970s, Guare "was depicted as an aspiring young dramatist whom critics assumed would follow in the footsteps of the masters of American drama: Eugene O'Neill, Arthur Miller, and Tennessee Williams" (11). Unlike many of his contemporaries, however, Guare forged his own trail by challenging much of what typified the conventional American theatrical form. If critics expected him to become America's next great mainstream playwright, they were mistaken. Instead in 2002 Guare was labeled—by Plunka—as "one of the most interesting and provocative, yet misunderstood, playwrights of the twentieth century" (13). Well into the twenty-first century, that assessment remains valid. By most measures, Guare's unconventional body of work is now largely recognized as one that has expanded the horizons and possibilities of the American theater, even if it has not precisely succeeded at altering the landscape. Realism still predominates the stage, and the "full" theater experience—including song and dance, direct address to audience, and other "fourth-wall" violations—remains more a curiosity than a commonplace happening. Still Guare persists in his pursuit of his own brand of American theatre.

Guare has actively studied American culture for a significant span of time, highlighting strengths and zoning in on weaknesses since the 1960s. Throughout an impressive and expansive career, he has maintained an enthusiasm for his craft, for the stage, and for the culture that offers him so much food for thought.

Guare is best known for *The House of Blue Leaves*, *Marco Polo Sings a Solo*, *Four Baboons Adoring the Sun*, and *Six Degrees of Separation*. His 2010 work, *A Free Man of Color*, extended his career into a sixth decade on the stage.

John Guare (pronounced either *gwār* or *gwâr*) was born 5 February 1938 in New York City, the only child to parents of Irish heritage (John Edward Guare and Helen Clare Grady), and raised a Roman Catholic in Jackson Heights, Queens. He composed neighborhood plays as early as 1949 and was actually written up in the local paper for his enterprise. His interest in entertainment is something of a family matter: Guare's great-uncles on his mother's side, Jimmy and Jere Grady, were vaudevillians performing highly theatrical melodramas of various sorts from 1880 to 1925. At times they even included a dwarf in the act, discovered in a cathouse raid by Guare's grandfather, a Lynn, Massachusetts, policeman. Before John was born, Guare's parents are reported to have loved the prank of hiding the dwarf, Billy Rhodes, in a baby carriage and surprising people who were expecting a sweet newborn rather than a cigar-smoking and raspy-voiced, though diminutive, adult. That kind of quirky sense of humor was present in the Guare household throughout John's upbringing and eventually found its way into his plays. Another of his uncles, "Big Bill," became an agent and head of casting at Metro-Goldwyn-Mayer from 1934 to 1956, representing W. C. Fields, Al Jolson, and Will Rogers and discovering James Stewart and Elizabeth Taylor, among others. "Big Bill" was not much of a physical presence in John's family life, being instead a sort of specter of success that haunted both of his parents to varying degrees, probably rising to mythic status precisely because of his physical absence. To that effect characters based on him appear in various Guare plays as symbols of an American success unfortunately unattainable by the vast majority of its aspirants.

Guare had the good fortune of being able to see Broadway plays—mostly musicals—almost every week during his childhood. That exposure, coupled with being a voracious reader, led him to feel at home in the theater. Early in his readings, he discovered Anton Chekhov's *Three Sisters,* and it powerfully evoked wistful emotions for him. In his mind he substituted New Orleans for Moscow, and as he reports in his preface for the collection of his plays *The War against the Kitchen Sink,* though he "couldn't get to New Orleans . . . [he] could get to the theater."[2] *Three Sisters* displays that rare Chekhovian blend of concrete realism and fragile sentimentalism, and it inspired the young Guare to try his hand at something similar. When he had his parents take him to the Tyrone Guthrie production of Christopher Marlowe's sixteenth-century *Tamburlaine the Great,* however, everything seemed to come together: "Tamburlaine stood on the stage of the Winter Garden, unrolled an enormous map of the world, and strode across it. That one image so overwhelmed me that I could no longer watch TV miniatures like the original *Marty* set in living rooms like mine" (vii).

Mesmerized by Guthrie's magical theater and uninspired by realists such as Paddy Chayefsky, Guare's tastes in theater were developing quickly. His response was unambiguous and resounding when John Osborne's much celebrated, "revolutionary" kitchen-sink masterpiece, *Look Back in Anger,* came to New York from London in 1957: "No! Not a kitchen sink! Where is the revolution?" (vii). The public excitement that preceded the play's American premiere was palpable, but disappointment was Guare's main reaction: "I despised plays with people sitting at kitchen tables pouring their hearts out and the people in the audience oohing when the people in the play turned on the faucet and real water came out. That kitchen sink. That was what I hated most" (vii).

Real revolution, according to Guare, *did* come a short time later from the pen of Osborne, but in the form of his less celebrated but far more theatrical *The Entertainer* (New York premiere 1958). It starred Laurence Olivier as an over-the-hill nightclub performer, who Guare reports "played out front to me as if I was not in New York, but in the audience of a shabby theater at a cheesy English seaside resort" (viii). The lesson Guare learned was that "the audience could play a role in the play. The audience was not a passive witness as it was in realistic, naturalistic plays, barred from the play by a brutal fourth wall" (viii). This was the sort of theater Guare wanted to create: poignant, funny, tragic. Before too long he found himself in the middle of the off-off-Broadway revolution of the 1960s, in which anti-kitchen-sink sentiment took firm root. Before the excitement of New York, however, Guare's college days did their part to shape his talents, and travel made an impression as well.

Guare left his beloved New York and went to Georgetown University in Washington, D.C., where he earned an English degree (B.A. 1960) and spent a great deal of his time polishing his youthful love of language by writing a play a year. In 1957 he won second place in a student playwriting contest with the comic parody *She Conqs to Stooper.* In 1958 he contributed a song to an original musical revue titled *The Natives Are Restless,* presented by the school's Mask and Bauble Dramatic Society. It was a college-wit-level comedy celebrating famous people whose names included the letter "o." In 1959 the Mask and Bauble produced *Thirties Girl,* Guare's play about Hollywood during the transition to talkies, dealing with the dethronement of a reigning silent-film diva by a fresh-faced, talking starlet. The play's songs later reappeared in *The House of Blue Leaves.* Guare's *The Toadstool Boy* won first place in the 1960 District of Columbia Recreation Department's one-act play competition, about a musician who commits suicide in order to generate a cult following. This plot idea also resurfaces in later work. And his love of the one-act play has never died, given how well it has served as a venue for experimentation.

Following his undergraduate years, Guare took his talents to New Haven, Connecticut and polished them further at the Yale School of Drama (MFA, 1963). In 1962 Yale produced Guare's one-act *The Golden Cherub,* with a main character drawing from Osborne's Jimmy Porter of *Look Back in Anger* fame. His 1963 three-act Yale University Theatre production, *Did You Write My Name in the Snow?,* is Guare's first full-length concentration on the absurd nature of the human condition. This theme has remained a focus throughout his professional career.

The level and caliber of education that Guare received stands in notable contrast to the educations of peers he eventually met in New York City. It is a contrast reflected in much of Guare's work, which generally exhibits an allusiveness and polish only infrequently found in the work of other American playwrights of his generation.

Guare could be said to have been discovered as a result of the 1963 *Did You Write My Name in the Snow?,* though it took a later rediscovery to send him on his professional way. On the strength of that production, he was offered a writing-trainee job in the film industry at Universal Studios. Guare's Uncle Billy arranged a similar offer at MGM, but a military draft notice interrupted his career. After a six-month stint in the Air Force Reserve, he resumed his plans to move to Hollywood, until an aunt from San Francisco intervened. Guare reports: "She had planned to leave me two thousand dollars. Now, she would give the sum to me if I left California, went back to New York, wrote plays, went to Europe, sent her postcards."[3] Already inclining toward the stage rather than the screen, Guare accepted his aunt's offer, returned to New York, and determined to place his future in the hands of living theater.

In 1965 Guare completed his agreement with his aunt by making a trip to Europe, attending theatrical performances in London, tossing his belongings in the Seine while in Paris, and hitchhiking to Istanbul and then Cairo, all the while writing about his experiences in his notebooks and on postcards. While in Cairo his parents sent him news of the Pope's visit to New York, prompting something of a revelation for Guare: "Sitting in Cairo, reading what that day meant to them back on Queens Boulevard, I saw my life and all our dreams and where those dreams had taken us, and I realized I had a subject. I started writing *House of Blue Leaves*" (89). Though he returned with parts of the play in hand, the path to success by way of *Blue Leaves* was not a short one. His father's death in July slowed any creative momentum Guare had. Several months later a reading of one act of the play at the Eugene O'Neill Memorial Theatre in Waterford, Connecticut, sparked interest and landed him an ABC Television grant to study film writing at Yale. The reading also caught the eye of a set of New York producers. Guare needed more time with the play, though, during which time he wrote *Something I'll Tell You Tuesday* (1965) and *The Loveliest Afternoon of the Year* (1965), two short plays that were performed at New York's famous Off-Off-Broadway venue Caffe Cino, both set in New York and both populated by souls desperate for meaningful contact.

Two longer works, *Muzeeka* (1968) and *Cop-Out* (1968), followed, the former a response to the idealist undergraduates Guare encountered while at Yale, the latter drawn from antiwar protests that he had witnessed and experienced, including an occasion when he personally was knocked unconscious in a protest altercation. *Muzeeka,* double-billed with Sam Shepard's *Red Cross,* squeezes one man's lifetime into an imaginative chronicle of hollow success, misdirected ambitions, and, ultimately, suicide, following a formula that could be described as Brechtian, episodic, and expressionistic. It won an Obie for best Off-Broadway play, Guare's first major award.

Cop-Out debuted at the Eugene O'Neill Memorial Theatre in Waterford in July 1968 and was later presented as part of a double bill with Guare's *Home*

Fires at New York's Cort Theatre. This first brush with Broadway, however, ended after four performances and a number of negative reviews (though later in the season it earned him the Most Promising Playwright Award from *Variety*). Devastated, Guare took off to Europe again. Finally, on his return to New York, he finished *The House of Blue Leaves,* inspired in part by seeing Olivier in London acting in plays by August Strindberg and Georges Feydeau on successive nights, which provided an insight into the potential interdependency of these two playwrights' different styles: "The savage intensity of the first blended into the maniacal intensity of the second. . . . Why shouldn't Strindberg and Feydeau get married, at least live together, and *The House of Blue Leaves* be their child?"[4]

The year 1971 was Guare's breakout year with *The House of Blue Leaves*. This domestic drama is at once wildly comic and despairing. It includes a nightclub wannabe not unlike Osborne's own washed up entertainer. Unlike Osborne's work, however, Guare's stage is overrun by strange and curious characters and comic insanity, literal and figurative: Guare inserts a band of groupie nuns, a deaf movie starlet, a plot to blow up the Pope, and dreams of moving to Hollywood. Amid all the hilarity, death makes a gruesome visit. Realistic around the edges but filled with significant nonrealistic eruptions, this theatrical curiosity won the New York Drama Critics' Circle Award for best American play and moved Guare into the front ranks of American dramatists.

During this same year, Guare's interest in theater that goes beyond the fourth wall extended to Central Park and the New York Shakespeare Festival, where his musical adaptation of Shakespeare's *Two Gentlemen of Verona* (cocreated with Mel Shapiro) was performed. Capturing the free spirit of 1960s–70s New York City, the play's hippie, free-living, antiwar enthusiasm was a big success, even including a much-acclaimed portable borough tour through the city. It transferred to Broadway, ran for 613 performances, and received the Drama Desk Award for outstanding musical, best book, and best lyrics. During this same period, Guare also received shared credit (with Milos Forman, Jean-Claude Carrière, and John Klein) for the script of the film *Taking Off* after director Forman asked him to work on script revisions. The film won the 1971 Cannes Film Festival Jury Prize. It was a successful year for Guare, to say the least.

The 1970s continued to be a busy time for Guare. *Marco Polo Sings a Solo* was first produced by the Nantucket Stage Company in 1973 and was revised and restaged at New York's Public Theatre. Set on an iceberg occupied by a group of characters whose extremely successful and highly unlikely careers mark them as giants in the mythic modern world they inhabit, the play reveals just how hollow their lives are. Somewhat reminiscent of Thornton Wilder's *The Skin of Our Teeth, Marco Polo* is richly theatrical and philosophically poetic. In 1977 *Landscape of the Body* (with songs by Mel Shapiro) opened in Chicago before moving to New York. Though less wildly imaginative than *Marco Polo,* it does include flashbacks and flash forwards as well as, most memorably, a dead character resurrected as the play's narrator who reveals information unavailable to the living in this play of gruesome crimes and lost souls. Although it won the Joseph Jefferson Award for playwriting, negative critical reaction once again upset Guare. As a result he decided to avoid New York venues and opened his next work, *Bosoms and Neglect* (1979), at Chicago's Goodman Theatre. The play returns to the kooky but desperate world of *Blue Leaves* in many respects, generating what may best be termed a new normal in a world that is comically out of joint. During the latter half of 1979, Guare worked with director Louis Malle writing the screenplay *Atlantic City,* a richly moody film about lost souls in a dying city. In a twist that is typical for Guare, moral certainty is pushed to its limit, and murder ultimately converts to a virtuous act. Guare was nominated for an Academy Award, and the film won numerous prizes, including the Golden Lion at the Venice Film Festival.

In 1981 Guare received the Award of Merit from the American Academy and Institute of Arts and Letters. That same year he married Adele Chatfield-Taylor, whom he had met six years earlier, and they took a month-long honeymoon in England. Chatfield-Taylor is an architect who served as head of the American Academy in Rome, the city that became Guare's second home for twenty-five years until Chatfield-Taylor stepped down in 2014.

In the early 1980s, family lineage and American heritage took hold of Guare's imagination, resulting in an ongoing project of writing and revision that is generally referred to as his tetralogy, a cycle of plays on nineteenth-century America collectively titled *Lydie Breeze.* Begun in 1981, the plays have been rewritten, recombined, and variously produced in parts and available wholes and have been performed in New York, Los Angeles, Chicago, San Francisco, Washington D.C., London, and Australia. Haunting and nearly mythic in its attachment to the American cataclysm that was the Civil War and the disillusioning decades that followed, *Lydie Breeze* traces the lives of war veterans turned idealists and utopians who are inevitably betrayed by their flawed humanity. The plays cast a forward glance to the twentieth century—the "American Century"—as Guare uses the benefit of hindsight to present a case that certain behavior within our country's history perhaps should have forewarned us of difficulties our dreams and illusions would create for future generations. In short these historically based dramas investigate the violence at the root of American identity and the failure of utopian aspirations in a style that differs from Guare's other works while capturing the same thematic mix of despair amid inextinguishable hope.

In 1981 Guare was also involved with Louis Malle again, this time collaborating on the film *Moon over Miami,* about the Federal Bureau of Investigation's Abscam sting, with John Belushi scheduled for the starring role. When Belushi unexpectedly died, Guare converted his text to a play and presented it at the Williamstown (Mass.) Theatre Festival (1987) and the Yale Repertory Theatre (1989). Smaller projects during the period included *Hey, Stay a While* (1984), a lobby-style program of Guare pieces for Chicago's Goodman Theatre; a short work on gluttony, part of a "Show of the Seven Deadly Sins" that was itself part of Nagle Jackson's *Faustus in Hell,* which premiered in 1985 at Princeton's McCarter Theatre; and *The Talking Dog,* an adaptation of a Chekhov short story, for an event (and book) titled *Orchards: A Chekhov Evening* commissioned by Anne Cattaneo of the Acting Company and taken on a sixty-city national tour that ended in New York. In 1986 Greg Mosher of New York's Lincoln Center revived *The House of Blue Leaves* (he originally wanted to do *Gardenia*—one of the parts of *Lydie Breeze*—but was unable to secure the desired cast) with an all-star cast that included John Mahoney, Ben Stiller, Stockard Channing, Swoosie Kurtz, and Christopher Walken, running for 420 performances and winning four Tonys. Guare's Lincoln Center connection was one that has continued to this day, with Guare premiering plays at the venue and serving as coeditor of the *Lincoln Center New Theater Review.*

Guare's biggest success to date occurred on the Lincoln Center stage (the Mitzi E. Newhouse Theater): *Six Degrees of Separation* (1990), an intricately plotted comedy of manners about an African American confidence man who poses as the son of film star Sidney Poitier and ensnares a well-heeled art salesman and his wife with his charms. Directed by Jerry Zaks (who directed the *Blue Leaves* revival) and starring again Stockard Channing—and later Swoosie Kurtz—the play won an Obie Award and the New York Drama Critics' Circle Award and was a finalist for the Pulitzer Prize in drama. It also was produced in London's Royal Court in 1992 and won an Olivier Award for best play. In 1993 it was made into a film, scripted by Guare, starring Channing, Donald Sutherland, and Will Smith. The play and film gained unsolicited publicity when Guare noted that the inspiration for the play came from a newspaper report of a sophisticated African American hustler who tricked the well-to-do. As a result of this passing comment, the trickster named in the article, David Hampton, located and pursued Guare in an effort to claim part of the play's and movie's earnings. This public, legally adjudicated conflict resulted in temporary notoriety for Hampton and an interesting footnote in the annals of New York theater.

Four Baboons Adoring the Sun (1992) followed, directed by Sir Peter Hall and performed at Lincoln Center's Vivian Beaumont Theater, once again with Stockard Channing. It is a family drama that raises the conventional to nearly archetypal levels by capturing the dysfunction of modern life against a backdrop of an Italian archaeological dig haunted by ancient spirits. *Chaucer in Rome* received its world premiere in 1999; it transports relatives of characters from *The House of Blue Leaves* to an expatriate existence in Rome, with results largely mirroring events from the earlier play. During its 1998–99 theater season, New York's Signature Theatre Company made Guare its annual playwright of focus (an honor extended to many of America's best-known, including Arthur Miller the preceding season) by producing *Marco Polo Sings a Solo* and *Bosoms and Neglect* and staging the world premiere of *Lake Hollywood* (1999). *Lake Hollywood* follows the unlikely machinations of several characters desperate for normalcy but also for the quick wealth of a real estate scheme that will involve the rich and famous as clients. *A Few Stout Individuals* followed in 2002, commissioned and produced by the Signature Theatre Company. Something of a by-product of Guare's 1980s history cycle, the play documents Ulysses S. Grant's final days of life following his disastrous presidency and scandalous business ventures. Deathly ill, Grant tries to complete his memoirs in order to correct history and restore his family's honor and financial fortunes. Mark Twain and the emperor of Japan are also characters in the play, yet another highly imaginative production of historical material that captures the heart of American culture during its formative stages.

A Free Man of Color (2010), another Lincoln Center production, may be Guare's most ambitious single play to date. A nominee for the Pulitzer Prize, this historically suggestive, highly theatrical play—epic in nature and perhaps a bit unwieldy as it pursues its agenda—is set in New Orleans as Guare imagines it to have been in 1802, on the verge of converting from Spanish to French to American hands, complete with all the cultural clashes and convergences that such freewheeling national and cultural identity changes would generate. The play is at once history lesson, farce, and sex comedy with a Restoration-theater flavor. Guare uses theatricality to suggest where and how America's Anglo-Puritan heritage and economic ambitions clashed with Spanish and French *joi de vivre* and unintentionally undermined the high ideals that the New World once aspired to attain.

In 2012 the McCarter Theatre in Princeton produced *Are You There, Mr. McPhee?*, a frenetic romp of unlikely connections arranged and controlled by a playwright, Mundie, retelling a tale set in 1975. A realist play spiced with absurdism, *Are You There, Mr. McPhee?* is Guare at his most freewheeling. The following year the Atlantic Theater Company staged Guare's *3 Kinds of Exile,* which also marked his professional acting debut. The work is a collection of three one-act pieces about Eastern European émigrés and engages issues of home and personal identity. Over the past decades Guare has maintained his interest in the one-act play, a form that permits the sorts of experimentation that have been the hallmark of his entire career. Some are autobiographical monologues (*What It Was Like,* 2010), while others (*Between,* 2014) are engaging short dialogues.

Guare has also been involved with music and musical theater beyond those elements that pop up in works such as *Two Gentlemen of Verona*. He wrote narration for *Psyche,* an 1888 symphonic tone poem by César Franck, which premiered at New York's Avery Fisher Hall, Lincoln Center, in October 1997, conducted by Kurt Masur with the New York Philharmonic. In 1999 he revised the book of the Cole Porter musical comedy *Kiss Me, Kate* for its Broadway revival. He also wrote the book for the 2002 Broadway musical *Sweet Smell of Success* starring John Lithgow.

Guare taught playwriting at the Yale School of Drama from 1981 to 1984 (including one class taught in tandem with Arthur Kopit and Derek Walcott), and at the invitation of drama school dean James Bundy, he again taught at Yale from 2004 to 2010. He also taught a class in 1991 for Robert Brustein at the American Repertory Theater in Cambridge, Massachusetts, and with Terrence McNally he started a graduate-level playwriting program at New York's Julliard School in 1995. In 2011 he returned to the classroom, teaching an undergraduate course at Princeton. His inexhaustible theatrical iconoclasm continues to endear him to young talent, whom he encourages to utilize the full arsenal of theatrical tools that he has used for more than six decades. In addition to his pedagogical activities and his coeditorship of the *Lincoln Center Theater Review*, Guare coproduces the New Plays Reading Room Series at the Lincoln Center Library for the Performing Arts.

Where does John Guare fit in the long and distinguished history of American theater? Casting a backward look over the past one hundred years reveals an art form dedicated essentially to the *anti*theatrical form of realism and its more intense relative, naturalism. The more accurately the stage seemingly duplicates reality, the better the theater was reported to be. Anything that hinted at actually being in the theater was somehow contrary to the aesthetic expectations of American critics and audiences. Playwrights are often remembered for the gutty realism they capture on the page, actors for methodically *becoming* the characters they portray, dialogue for capturing the nearly inarticulate patterns of daily interaction, and sets for their familiar domesticity. Anything "theatrical," anything that toys with or undermines an audience's ability to exercise the willing suspension of disbelief, was viewed with suspicion. If an actor breaks the fourth wall by directly addressing the audience, if music or song or poetic language is employed, if anything other than straight chronology structures the play, if anything other than straightforward storytelling is the playwright's goal, then the play risks censure or even outright rejection.

This is not to say that some very good American theater has strayed off the realist path, but notable examples of such have been largely exceptions that prove the rule. For the most part, the greatest favor, honor, and attention traditionally have gone to realist masterworks. It seems a curiosity that so many talented people, for such a long period, would dedicate themselves to the theater and then so willingly discard many tools of its trade, to the point that the ultimate goal of "good" theater was taken to be anything but theatrical.

John Guare is an American playwright who not only noted this curiosity at an early stage in his development but also chose to do something about it. His theater is realistic when it needs to be but not to the extent that it sacrifices all else in order to preserve the fourth wall illusion and realistic credibility. In many instances Guar actively works to break through the fourth wall, to ignore Aristotelian prescriptions of beginnings, middles, and ends, and to present events indebted to the traditions of forms *other* than realist/naturalist theater. The kitchen sink ethos and the gloomy domestic settings around that sink are the points of contention in Guare's self-proclaimed war against realism. His is what he calls a struggle to restore "the theater to its true nature as a place of poetry, song, joy, a place of darkness where the bright truth is told."[5] Speaking of *Four Baboons Adoring the Sun* in particular, director Sir Peter Hall observed of Guare in general that "he uses theater boldly and in a thoroughly post-naturalistic way. His plays, with their combination of direct audience address, sudden time shifts, and vivid metaphorical emblems, rely on the sensibility of an age conditioned by jump cuts and dissolves of the cinema. Yet his work is quintessentially of the theater. . . . He needs a live audience to make it work."[6]

In this same vein, Guare acknowledges a keen debt from early in his career to William Shakespeare. In a 2011 interview, reflecting on his musical adaptation of Shakespeare's *Two Gentlemen of Verona,* Guare observed:

> I went to London in 1965 and saw a series of Shakespeare productions that were just revelations. . . . The main lesson I learned from Shakespeare early on was that he had no stage directions. . . . You had to pack the line, and the line had to do the work of the set, the costume and the lights. . . . I had always loathed all the stage directions in O'Neill and Shaw. I loved the plays, but I hated the stage directions. I love the way that Shakespeare does it. The only lesson—to me, the most important lesson of playwriting—is that the line has to contain everything. What I love about Shakespeare is that he writes his subtext. The subtext is always visible. He strangely demands

> clarity of thought. The beauty and density of the language can blind people to its meaning, but as Sir Peter Hall once said to me, you can find a declarative sentence in every speech that tells you what the sense of that particular moment is. . . . It's both the clarity and the shameless theatricality of it. I must always remember to write my play as if it is to be done on a bare stage and the line has to carry everything.[7]

Guare's strategy is to overwhelm modern American theater's longstanding tradition of realism by breaking into song and dance, venturing into fantasy worlds, and offering cabaret-style monologues, soliloquies, jokes, and one-liners. As Hall notes, it is more than reasonable to assume contemporary audiences trained by watching movies are equipped to handle this new theatricality. It also seems reasonable to suggest that theater has much more to offer than a strategy of presenting faithful journalistic or photographic depictions of the world just outside the auditorium. Guare takes these points as his foundation by creating an engaging, often challenging, generally thoughtful, and invariably entertaining theater that is by no means characteristic of the traditional American stage.

Entertaining as they often are, Guare's plays utilize theater's tricks of the trade for purposes other than mere entertainment. For Guare form is integral to function, and in his case challenging the form of realism is to challenge its implicit endorsement of Western culture's Enlightenment-based worldview, especially faith in reason and logical progression. Writing in particular of Guare's *Six Degrees of Separation,* Mike Vanden Heuvel observes of the work that it "offers more than the liberal bourgeois ethic of social unity achieved through more efficient communication."[8] The purport of this ethic, Vanden Heuvel argues, is that close observation of reality coupled with rational analysis will lead to human advancement and demolition of all obstacles to happiness. This position holds sway even today over a large swath of Western cultural thought, though it has lost its nearly monolithic acceptance, at least since World War II (and more likely since the catastrophe of World War I). For Guare reason is not the weapon of mass social unification it was once thought to be. Solutions to world crises may be insurmountable if we choose to use reason alone. This is Guare's fear. But he moves beyond that fear and converts this fear into a celebration of precivilized foundations in human nature. He chooses to look at this untamed and untamable part of human nature with an honesty he feels has not been properly studied by a world invested in rational enlightenment. For Guare rationalist-based realism is not just unexciting theater; it actually encourages foolhardy, dangerous, and often cataclysmic ways of seeing the world.

The European absurdists of the mid-twentieth century—and other notables before them—tapped into an antirationalist vein that captured the imagination of a decimated post–World War II Europe.[9] Absurdism was less of a gripping phenomenon, however, in the United States. To a large degree, Guare's theater is an American version of European absurdism, though his is not as utterly iconoclastic as much of the work of those nearly nihilistic European playwrights.

This American movement began during the adventurous theatrical heyday of New York in the 1960s. In venues far from Broadway sprung up a youthful reaction against the stultifying obsession with realist convention. Experimentalism found a home in unusual venues, where young playwrights found places to try almost anything in front of live (but usually small) audiences. Larger venues and larger paychecks eventually lured many of these young and talented practitioners. With them curious hybridizations of realism and theatrical experimentation followed onto these brighter stages.

Guare was one such playwright: he challenged everything he felt was wrong with the kitchen sink way of thinking about the world and its problems. Unlike many of his early contemporaries, however, he has continued to commission high theatricality to reveal an acute sense of the failure of human relations in an increasingly posthuman world dedicated to the pursuit of the sorts of lifestyles that lack any significant nutritional value, spiritual and otherwise. Probing and quite critical of contemporary American culture, Guare uses his theater to open audiences to the possibilities of change that may exist beyond rationalist-based prescriptions. In the process he identifies the chains of bleak inevitability that are the grim hallmarks of the realist/naturalist tradition. Hard work and moral rectitude are not guarantees of success or happiness. The good do not always win, and evil seems forever ascendant. Guare refuses to see episodes of failed rationalism as proof of unending human misery in general, however. From the embers of his often bleak stage invariably rise signals of hope—even laughter and joy—somehow beyond the bounds of logic, reason, or common sense.

CHAPTER 2

Early Work

Even though Guare reports that *The House of Blue Leaves,* first staged in 1971, was the work where he finally discovered himself as playwright, his earlier works of the 1960s already demonstrated pretty clearly that his professional trajectory would not be the traditional one of writing in the realistic or naturalistic vein. His love of music, vaudevillian variety, audience engagement, and episodic vignettes promised a theater that differed from standard American mainstream fare. As his college work foretold, experimentation and full theatricality have been Guare's hallmark throughout his long career. He is one of a very few playwrights whose artistic ideals successfully resisted commercial pressures to compromise.

Like many playwrights of his generation, Guare took an early interest in one-act plays, given their relative ease to produce (compared to the behind-the-scenes work required to mount a full-length play) and reduced pressure to be profitable. Experimentation is better undertaken under the commercial radar, and one-act plays permit this freedom to a greater degree. Unlike many of Guare's contemporaries, however, his interest in one-act plays—and the reasons behind that interest—has stayed with him to the present day.

On 25 October 1966, Caffe Cino in New York City premiered a double bill of Guare's two one-acts *Something I'll Tell You Tuesday* and *The Loveliest Afternoon of the Year.* That Guare was produced at the famous Caffe Cino—birthplace of the Off-Off-Broadway theater movement—was for him a badge of honor in itself, given that it was a place where many other young playwrights, Sam Shepard and Lanford Wilson among them, found their first audiences. The two plays are set in New York and separately exhibit the sort of contemporary urban alienation that would be a mainstay of many of Guare's more mature works in one form or another.

Something I'll Tell You Tuesday is a generational piece, with an elderly husband, Andrew, preparing to take his wife, Agnes, to the hospital, waiting for their daughter and son-in-law to arrive from New Jersey to help them out. The younger couple, Hildegarde and George, enter the apartment spewing vile insults and murderous threats against each other, leaving the audience to cringe along with the elderly couple as the scene unfolds. Two crucial elements prevent this play from falling into the category of conventional kitchen sink realism. The first is Guare's use of scene changes, from apartment to hallway to restaurant in quick succession and with minimal sets. The rapid shifts and necessarily spare sets acknowledged the budget constraints of the Off-Off-Broadway venue, but they also demonstrated that Guare felt no need to duplicate the claustrophobic clutter of naturalism. For him sets need to change quickly in order to maintain an entertaining (i.e., theatrical) pace. So rather than relying on a realistic set to convey stifling entrapment, he works to have his dialogue be the mechanism that closes in on his elderly victims—and his audience—in a manner that he credits as having learned from Shakespeare's theater. The aggression displayed by the younger couple is palpable and the sense of entrapment real thanks to their inhuman verbal assaults throughout the piece. The second difference involves Guare's unwillingness to succumb to the idea of linear inexorability that is standard naturalist/realist procedure. Typically naturalist or realist plays weigh in on their characters in a way that implies the trajectory of their lives is unchangeable and inevitable. Guare, however, ends the play with an unexpected twist, an enlightening surprise that undermines an audience's traditionalist expectations. Turning back to the play's title, he has the elderly mother ask her husband to remind her to tell her daughter that they should be happy with their fighting because some day—like the elderly couple—they will become too tired to carry on as they do, and the ensuing indifference is far worse than what the young couple currently have.

The twist is almost shocking, for the play sets up a conventional contrast between the supposedly idyllic past of the elderly couple when they were young and the blighted present of the current young couple. Instead what the audience sees is a continuum of a single marriage type, with the young couple representing what the old couple once was and the old couple suggesting what the young couple will eventually become. This falls in line as a reasonable alternative outcome, mildly unexpected but not terribly surprising. What *is* surprising, however, is how Guare reverses expectations by noting that the elder couple's "peace" is little more than elder apathy, a sad but apparently inevitable end to life, an unsettling peace that precedes death. As unnerving as it may be, youthful bile beats what the young couple can expect with the onset of their "golden years." As unsavory as Guare makes the young couple, having them assault the audience's sensibilities in many negative ways, he suggests that these are the best years of marriage. The play presents a clearly bleak picture of married life. When it comes to craft, however, Guare manages to create something that steps beyond standard expectation, and that is what one finds is truly worthy of note in this play.

The Loveliest Afternoon of the Year involves a city park encounter between HE and SHE, HE chastising SHE for feeding the pigeons, SHE afraid that HE is a mugger. The two settle into conversation, with HE giving the standard "I'm the misunderstood husband" story, presumably in an attempt to gain sympathy and curry sexual favors. Standard fare. HE, however, tells a hilariously absurd and anything but macho tale: "My wife takes all my money and she bends it in her teeth so I can't use it. I have to walk everywhere because she bends all my subway tokens. And she has a blue rifle with a silencer on it and shoots my feet so I have to dance this crazy darting dance whenever I come in late."[1] His frankly unbelievable tales have a charm that attracts SHE, including one involving his sister, Lucy, who lost an arm to a polar bear, which grew back. But she also grew polar bear fur, forcing her to move to Alaska. Guare's vivid imagination is on display here, a definite sign of things to come, but what catches the theatergoer in this work, in addition to its linguistic facility, is the author's use of stage techniques such as direct audience address, songs to advance plot and mood, and flashbacks breaking with straight chronology, all ingenious bits of theater that keep the play moving briskly without pause. Through all these entertaining storytelling devices, the plot turns as expected: the meeting turns into an affair. There remains the one issue, however, namely that SHE—and the audience—is never quite certain whether HE is a pathological but entertaining and charming liar or may perhaps be telling the straight though incredible truth. The play's final moment changes everything when the wife appears with a blue rifle and shoots the lovers. SHE is doubly amazed—as is the audience—first by her mortal wound and second to find out that her lover's strange tales were not invented at all: "Hey, you really do have a sister Lucy, don't you?" (102). Real life, it turns out, can be stranger than fiction, making truth and fantasy sometimes impossible to distinguish. Guare has made this point throughout his career with sometimes chilling effect, as is the case in this play. Fantastic and imaginative tales may be entertaining, but there is something unsettling and even sinister when the fantastic turns out to be cut from reality itself.

The double-bill did receive a minor review from the *Village Voice,* which criticized *Something I'll Tell You Tuesday* for being part of an Off-Off-Broadway trend toward realism without purpose and *The Loveliest Afternoon of the Year* as just another black comedy imitation of Edward Albee's *The*

Zoo Story.[2] While both points may be partly true, it is not necessarily the case that they warrant negative criticism; rather they indicate Guare's participation in a youth movement working to set its own standards. It should also be added that Guare has often commented that Off-Off-Broadway experimentation became less of a joy once critical scrutiny became part of the production formula.

A Day for Surprises is not likely to have been drawn from true events, at least not in any literal sense, though the pathetic truth of the characters bubbles through the dramatic flight of fancy that Guare creates. Also a Caffe Cino production (August 1967, though given an earlier open night production at Theatre Genesis), this one-act involves two New York Public Library librarians, labeled A (a female, also referred to as Miss Jepson) and B (a male, also referred to as Mr. Falanzano), desperately searching for human contact in a cold, empty world. A and B are burdened with the added inconvenience of being generally ill equipped to make meaningful contact in even the best of situations. The day's first surprise starts the action: one of the stone lion statues guarding the library's entrance is missing. It winds up being sighted prowling in a nearby ladies' room and has apparently eaten a Miss Pringle. B surprises A with news that he and Miss Pringle were engaged to be married. His story includes further surprises, tales of sex in the stacks and an unwanted pregnancy. A is enthralled by the emotions that these revelations stir in her, generating a parallel between her awakening from a stultifying life of routine and the lion itself transforming from inanimate stone to dangerous life. But the librarian in her never quite evaporates. Using library paste to glue herself to B, she binds the two of them in the only bond she seems to comprehend. The stone lion returns to its perch, and B sings a song likely drawn from a favorite book, leaving some doubt about the pair's ability to remain truly among the living. This play, as much as any Guare had written to this point, introduces an essential recurring theme: the need to invigorate existences threatened by routine. What makes Guare truly distinct is that this thematic inclination is a dramaturgical one as well. Gene A. Plunka observes that "the form of his plays matches the content: what begins as realism is suspended from its inertia by Guare's absurd view of life, in which surprise turns conventional drama into something more creative and imaginative."[3] *A Day for Surprises* has the added distinction of being the first of several Guare plays to have characters experience life through books, Guare's *Bosoms and Neglect* being the most notable example.

Moving beyond realism with even greater verve than before, Guare next wrote *Muzeeka,* which opened 10 October 1967 at the Los Angeles Mark Taper Forum. On 28 April 1968 it opened in New York's Provincetown Playhouse, double-billed with Sam Shepard's *Red Cross,* marking Guare's first professional contact with mainstream New York theater, including his first contact with major New York media. The play imaginatively breaks the inertia of realism by creating six scenes reminiscent of Bertolt Brecht's epic theater and the expressionist traditions of early twentieth-century European playwrights. The scenes present Jack Argue (an anagram of *Guare*) in a descent from youthful first-job hopefulness to despairing suicide. Jack's inner state, rather than his external circumstances, takes center stage by way of a minimal set, stagehands occupying the space to assist Jack in his storytelling, banners announcing one event after another, songs capturing states of emotion, and blackouts vigorously bridging one episode to another. Longing for a life of harmony, Argue proclaims his desire to be like the ancient Etruscans (drawing from Guare's early travels through Italy), whose mysterious pre-Roman culture left nothing except tantalizing archaeological hints that they were obsessed with dance. Says Argue, "A whole civilization dancing. Every part of them dancing. . . . And these smiles—these lovely, looney smiles—that should make them look like a race of Alfred E. Neumans except only genius could know the joy that's painted on those pots and bottles and urns."[4] Determined to convert the modern world by resurrecting this same joy of dance, Argue hires on with Muzak in hopes of taking that mind-numbing elevator music and "pip[ing] in my own secret music that I keep hidden here under my cortical overlay and I'll free all the Etruscans in all our brains" (7). This biggest of dreams is thwarted by the realities of contemporary life, including conventions of work and demands of domesticity. Conscription into the Vietnam War interrupts Argue's life, revealing the war to him in the same way that many Americans of the time saw that conflict, as a massive media event that fed a pathological thirst for blood and death. Generating a pervasive feeling of emptiness, the play is Guare's first to confront headlong the notion that the American dream is more nightmare than fairy tale. Even Argue's wife (in a letter to him) describes the dream in a way that is inadvertently unsavory and even grotesque: "The baby grew another foot today and I've enrolled her in dancing class already and I've enrolled him already in prep school because it can never be too early and I tell the baby everyday his daddy is a hero and fighting all those dirty commies in Vietnam so he can come home to us and make more money for us so we can move to a bigger house and go to Yale to college and Europe on vacations and take mommy to dances and plays and the club" (24).

It is a world where "God is on everybody's side" (24), where it seems everyone is happy. The clear feeling of emptiness, however, is unavoidable for any but the truly mindless. Amid the meaninglessness of it all, Argue stabs himself but lingers on stage through a raucous musical number that, like Muzak itself, is mind-numbingly patriotic, pro-American, and pro-Christian:

Hubert Humphrey
& Jesus Christ
Ronald Reagan
& Jesus Christ
Stokely Carmichael
& Jesus Christ
General Westmoreland
& Jesus Christ . . .
LBJ
Was Jesus Christ. . . . (24)

The names go on for some time (a stage direction specifies that "whatever names are in the news that day . . . should be used" [25]), with stagehands enthusiastically joining in. When the song breaks off, a character (labeled #2) offers a testimonial of Muzeeka's virtues, that it is like "a pink baby's backside poking up in the horizon and the air smells clean and it starts to rain and rain and the music never mounts, never builds, just stays stardustily in one mood and you love being alive" (25). All is spoken with no one aware that Argue is dead.

For Argue living ended well before his life concluded, and the same can be said for the events Guare has put on stage. Song and dance are definitely animated, but there is nothing of substance, nothing "Etruscan" among all the hollow sparkle and room-filling elevator music that "stays stardustily in one mood" until the final blackout.

Muzeeka won Guare an Off-Broadway Theater (Obie) Award, his first major theater award. J. K. Curry indicates that reviews "were mixed and seemed to vary according to how much the individual reviewer liked Off-Off-Broadway experimentation," indicating a general trend in Guare's critical reception.[5] Some saw the play as inventive and poetic, while others struggled to discover meaning. Alan Bunce of the *Christian Science Monitor* noted with approval that *Muzeeka* comprised "several quick, often incisive serio-comic scenes," while, less positively, Richard Hummler of *Variety* observed that the play offers "an expressionistic hodgepodge of familiar bop-the-bourgeoisie material."[6] Several noted the similarities between this work and Jean-Claude van Itallie's *America Hurrah,* an inventive piece developed by the experimental and influential Open Theatre. Among them was Jerry Tallmer of the *New York Post,* who saw the similarities but noted that Guare's work contained "its own mode of humor and point of view."[7] Edith Oliver of the *New Yorker* (more attuned to Broadway than Off-Off Broadway) complained that Guare's comic flare was "muffled" by his use of self-conscious "Brechtian tricks."[8]

In 1969, with his next work, *Cop-Out*—paired with his curtain-raiser *Home Fires*—Guare made it to Broadway (at the Cort Theatre), but the production ran for only eight performances, with many saying the play would have been better served by a smaller non-Broadway venue. *Cop-Out* was inspired by Guare's antiwar protest experiences. In 1968 he was accidentally knocked unconscious by a crowd-control police officer on horseback. When he came to, he saw nothing but "scared decent people on both sides. They might have shared a cup of coffee and a story together in another place, another time."[9] The play begins in darkness with piped-in Billie Holiday music, until bright lights flood the stage and reveal THE POLICEMAN, who begins a monologue about his first childhood memory, involving his dad and a police matter. The policeman then transforms into Brett Arrow, and events turn into comic-book fantasy as Arrow, sleuth extraordinaire, determines to capture the evil Mr. Big. Highly stylized scenes follow Arrow's progress as a Sam Spade imitation. In contrast a parallel set of interconnecting scenes reveals a growing romance between the policeman and an idealistic antiwar protester, THE GIRL, who meet while occupying opposite sides of a police barricade. The series of vignettes ultimately cohere as a tale of self-inflicted loneliness on the part of Arrow and the girl. A deceptive, pathetic life of the imagination absorbs too much of the policeman's energy and corrupts his vision of how the world operates, to the point that, at risk of losing a shot at promotion, he decides to abandon his growing love for the girl. The play turns even more desperate, closing with his shooting the girl to distance himself from affiliation with the other side, which he considers the main reason for failing to be promoted. In a rather sensationalist move, Guare has the girl die in the aisle of the theater, forcing the audience to step over the actress's prone body.

Studying how real life is corrupted by the fantasy worlds of B movies and blending theater styles to help him advance his themes are concerns Guare has continued to pursue in his career. The bold effort to confront and confuse his audience with the aisle-blocking corpse of the girl (played by Linda Lavin in the first production) is the sort of surprise that can be found throughout Guare's body of work. Though not always well received by the critics, Guare's plays continue to devise and implement theatrical novelties in his self-proclaimed "war against the kitchen sink," that mode of drama that Guare holds responsible for stifling the theatrical imagination even, ironically, as theater mourns the loss of creativity and imagination in the world at large.

The urge for conformity is one of the obstacles to a better, more creative world, a point Guare addresses in *Home Fires, Cop-Out*'s curtain raiser. *Home Fires* is a tale of patriotism set in a funeral parlor in Swampscott, "the gateway to New England," around the end of World War I.[10] A family of German descent, the Smiths (formerly the Schmidts), who have done everything they can to hide their heritage in this time of anti-German sentiment, are quietly mourning their family matriarch. Next door, heard but not seen, is the funeral of an Irish family, far less restrained in ceremony than their German counterparts. The funeral director has a strong feeling that the Smiths are in fact German but has no proof and so remains merely suspicious. One of the children of the deceased woman brings his outsider wife to the event. She is impeccably overdressed and apparently some sort of celebrity. Her star status is literally highlighted as she makes her entrance amid an unexpected, highly theatrical rain of lights and fanfare, signaling an obsession with fame that Guare identifies as the tinsel that destroys the substance of life. Her husband, Rudy (modeled loosely after Guare's Uncle Billy), is a talent agent who has climbed socially but remains mortified that his ancestry will destroy his ambitions. Instead his own gullibility will be his undoing.

The deceased woman is about to be buried with a prized ruby ring, and everyone's response to this fact reveals their character. Rudy wants to keep the ring in order to enhance his social standing. His father wants it in order to gain enough cash to attract an American second wife and confirm himself as an American once and for all. But Rudy's sister, Nell, the only family member actually born in the United States, grabs the ring and announces, "I'm going to hock it and sail back to Germany and find my name and find my relatives and apologize to them for losing the war and become Nell Schmidt again" (40). The closing scene is memorable, involving a rising and falling curtain that reveals a "frozen tableau of general confusion" as "marching bands in the street play joyfully" (44), celebrating America's victory over the Huns. Clearly America, obsessed with empty materiality, may win wars against tyranny and oppression, but it offers something far less than what it advertises, insisting on a conformity that calls into question its status as "land of the free."

This twin bill received numerous mainstream reviews that conceded confusion more than distaste. Clive Barnes of the *New York Times* was typical in enjoying the plays' humor despite their failure to connect to real life and make meaningful points.[11] Though the production closed after only eight performances, the exposure it provided was sufficient to earn Guare recognition as 1969's most promising playwright in a poll of New York drama critics conducted by *Variety*.

The last play to precede Guare's breakout play, *The House of Blue Leaves*, was a one-act television play, *Kissing Sweet*, commissioned by New York's Channel Thirteen as a part of a group of plays about pollution collectively titled *FOUL!*. Ten Off-Broadway writers were asked to contribute. The work aired in November 1969. Guare's contribution has two actors and two actresses playing multiple roles as each vignette quickly folds into another. The various scenes are commercial messages for products designed to clean up that most polluted product of all, the human body: "More products. More Sprays. More Pills. More creams. More soaps. We all have to pitch in. Bathe. Spray. Buy. Rid ourselves of our smells and sweats that spew their evil poisons into the skies. Scrub ourselves until nothing is left."[12] As the pitches drag on, stagehands pile a growing mound of junk onstage until the actors are completely overwhelmed. Guare's own "commercial" message: playing on people's discontentment with their natural selves and insecurities about who they are in general is a primary commercial strategy leading to a consumerism that overwhelms not only social resources but also any psychology of personal satisfaction that society might ever have had. What we do to our environment is damaging enough. Even more damaging, Guare suggests, is what society does to its individuals.

Plunka aptly sums up Guare's career to this stage by noting that "these early plays provide a preview of Guare's ironic sense of black humor" as well as "the foundation for the development of the social issues" that have continued to interested the playwright. These works "allowed Guare to experiment with the stage devices . . . that make him a uniquely gifted theatrical innovator" (68). Having explored a range of interests from the popular obsessions of the cult of celebrity to people's increasing inability to connect with fellow human beings, tragicomically conveying them by way of high theatricality, Guare coalesced the lessons of his "apprenticeship" in his first triumph.

CHAPTER 3

The House of Blue Leaves (1971) and *Two Gentlemen of Verona* (1971)

Guare's first professionally produced full-length play, *The House of Blues Leaves,* was relatively long in the making. On 4 October 1965, Pope Paul VI visited New York City to plead before the United Nations for, among other things, peace in Vietnam. The visit, which included a papal mass in Yankee Stadium, contained all the ingredients of a celebrity-inspired frenzy reminiscent of the Beatles' first visit to the United States less than two years earlier. Guare, however, was not in New York to experience the Pope's visit; having gone to Europe, he was in Rome, coincidentally, on October 4. He received a letter from his parents describing the papal visit shortly thereafter, while in Egypt. The visit, and his parents' letter about it in particular, inspired Guare to draft the first act of *House of Blue Leaves* in short order. In the summer of 1966, that first act was given a staged reading at the Eugene O'Neill Memorial Theatre Playwrights' Conference in Waterford, Connecticut, but Guare's father died that summer, and Guare lost the impetus to complete the play. In 1969, after a second trip to Europe—when he saw Olivier star in a realist play and then a farce on back-to-back nights—Guare was convinced that realism and farce could coalesce into effective theater, and he completed the second act of *House of Blue Leaves* with that conviction in mind.

While the play is frequently kooky, much of it is drawn from actual experience, supporting Guare's case that fact is often stranger than fiction. Guare did have an uncle who was a successful Hollywood power broker, and he did suffer the personal humiliation of "auditioning" for his uncle for the role of Huck Finn in the manner reported by the wayward son in the play. He could also draw on his school-day experiences with Roman Catholic nuns who were hungry to meet the Pope in Rome or even at home in New York. Guare was by no means committed to creating a conventional realist play from these facts, however.

To mount a successful major production that was decidedly nonrealistic in many of its characteristics, Guare needed to overcome the orthodoxy of realism among New York stage directors, actors, designers, and the like, who were just as committed to the form as most of the playwrights of the day. Any playwright who wrote in a nonrealist mode needed to be aware of all the elements needed to transform the text on the stage. This time, equipped with his earlier Broadway experiences, Guare was more cautious about how his play would be staged and whom he would trust to coordinate and direct the production. The initial director for *House of Blue Leaves* had also directed *Cop-Out/Home Fires,* Guare's unsuccessful Broadway debut. Determined not to repeat the same mistake twice, he and his producers recruited Mel Shapiro for the play's Off-Broadway premiere. Shapiro and Guare developed a production strategy that moved away from straight realism and toward the farce the playwright had envisioned.

Crucial to an understanding of *House of Blue Leaves* is Guare's prefatory observation: "Chekhov says we must never humiliate one another, and I think avoiding humiliation is the core of tragedy and comedy and probably of our lives."[1] This theme reverberates throughout Guare's canon, given that so much of his work centers on tales of frightened and confused individuals doing their best to shield themselves from humiliation.

The play begins before the house lights go down and curtain is drawn, with Artie Shaughnessy walking to a piano and asking the arriving audience to settle into their seats so he can begin his cabaret act. He plays several poor, self-authored imitations of show tunes, the audience (since it is not yet "showtime") never quite settles in, and Artie is upset that he has been so shabbily treated. This opening is telling. The dream of stardom seems in part to require at least some degree of talent, and Artie seems not to have it. This fact does not deter him, however, convinced as he is that persistence and one good break are the recipe for success. Guare suggests that the idea of the big break is one of the major delusions that holds together the persistent faith in the American dream. Throughout the play Artie and those around him work primarily under the premise that fame feeds fame. Chasing special anointment is a cornerstone of the American dream, and anything short of that anointed recognition spells doom, leading to oblivion, a fate worse than death. Artie's uncle, Billy Einhorn ("unicorn"), is a Hollywood talent agent from the neighborhood who is Artie's big hope for escape, recognition, and fame. As much as people in the play believe that the Pope can dispense good fortune among his flock—blessing Artie's sheet music, for example—it is Einhorn, representing Hollywood, who holds the real power in the play.

Artie is an everyman, dreaming of being discovered and let out of the stifling cage that is his life. The set reflects this sense of entrapment, including barred windows and a multiply locked front door. Artie, a professional zookeeper, complains: "Work all day in a Zoo. Come home to a zoo" (30). He is married to Bananas, a woman whose actions fit her nickname and whom Artie treats as a helpless, trapped animal, feeding, medicating, and attending to her as she loses control of her sanity. As strangely as she behaves, she may be the one sane person in the play, though that is only dimly apparent on occasions such as when she reveals mild contempt for the cult of celebrity: "I like animals. You know why? I never heard of a famous animal" (30). Artie's son, Ronnie, is another lost soul, scarred by the childhood humiliation of having performed a madcap audition before his uncle for the role of Huck Finn (mirroring the audition that so embarrassed Guare in real life during his own youth), after which Uncle Billy says to Artie: "You never told me I had an idiot for a godchild" (53). Ronnie is a failure in everyone's eyes, especially his father's, who dreams that his son will someday become Pope and give Artie the monopoly on church music. The dream is delusional, of course, but it indicates the extremes to which Ronnie would have to go to please his father. Guare has elsewhere made the interesting point—not readily apparent in the play itself—that if Artie had invested his energies in his family rather than in his impossible dreams, perhaps this family would not be so dysfunctional: "Their dreams of the future and outside the house were greater than their ability to enjoy what was right there in the house."[2]

Artie, Bananas, and Ronnie are all victims of a common misinterpretation of the American dream, that if one can dream it, it will happen. Even the Pope, in his Yankee Stadium address, provides a reasonable but easily misinterpreted summary of the conventional vision of American exceptionalism:

> We feel, too, that the entire American people is here present with its noblest and most characteristic traits: a people basing its conception of life on spiritual values, on a religious sense, on freedom, on loyalty, on work, on the respect of duty, on family affection, on generosity and courage. . . .—safeguarding the American spirit from those dangers which prosperity itself can entail and which the materialism of our day can make even more menacing. . . . From its brief but heroic history, this young and flourishing country can derive lofty and convincing examples to encourage us all in its future progress. (71–72)

The Pope's message sums up American virtues that, if properly exercised, could lead to a better world. These same virtues that have created the country's prosperity now threaten its continued progress, however, through misplaced vanity, isolated, individualized self-interest, and general misinterpretation. Prosperity remains the goal, but Guare warns against the "menace" of greed and blind ambition, qualities that are progressive virtues taken to their extreme. The way to prosperity has been complicated by feelings of entitlement leading to schemes for instant wealth or fame rather than hopes for an honest and dutiful life of decent values. Excess has taken over as the dominant American aspiration.

Thus the play's aspiring American family comprises Artie the zookeeper/dreamer, Bananas the harmlessly batty wife, and Ronnie the disappointing and disappointed son. Ronnie recently enlisted in the military but has gone AWOL and has secretly returned home. To fulfill his own quirky dream, he has decided on fame through infamy by blowing up the Pope and taking all the credit by declaring himself an orphan.

Into this world steps a force of nature, Bunny Flingus, a not unattractive thirty-something downstairs neighbor who has been educated by gossip columns, talk shows, and *Reader's Digest* and whose experiences in life include myriad jobs ranging from travel agent to legal assistant, qualifying her as specialist in any number of fields. She is the kind of person who defines suffering in movie-magazine terms, retelling the horror Sandra Dee survived when she realized she forgot her hair curlers on the eve of her first big screen test. As her name implies, Bunny Flingus is free with her sexual favors, but Guare adds the curiously comic twist that she is bad in bed and everyone knows it, mainly because she tells everyone. In lieu of sex, she uses her self-reported culinary prowess to tantalize and seduce, teasing Artie with sumptuous descriptions of food she will prepare once they marry. Selling a dream of what the future holds is a trick Bunny has learned to use in order to ensnare her man. Apparently it little matters what is used as bait—sex is the standard but by no means only attractor—if the strategy is well managed.

Until she meets Artie, Bunny has not met the man who has any chance of whisking her into the fantasyland of celebrity status that she longs for. She can sing Artie's praises and be his muse without any concern for his real talent because the avenue to success is his connection to Einhorn, whom she hopes will put him on the road to Hollywood stardom. Where Bananas asks Artie to play certain songs she likes, Bunny loves everything indiscriminately, bent on propping up her future meal ticket with clichés and empty compliments. On the morning of the Pope's visit, she pushes Artie to make the call to Hollywood, though the call is less promising than she had hoped.

Bunny also succeeds in getting Artie to make final arrangements to get Bananas committed to an asylum. He describes the grounds of the asylum in almost poetic terms, the result of his having seen a tree covered with bluebirds that he mistook for blue leaves. If the asylum can be described as a house of blue leaves, so too can Artie's house, and maybe the entire theater as well. The madhouse that is Bananas's intended destination is right before the audience's eyes; no need to relocate her.

Act 1 could be described as a quirky realist play, setting up Artie, Bunny, and Bananas as plausible though unlikely character studies. Act 2 starts out reasonably enough, with Ronnie secretively entering with a suspicious package and directly addressing the audience (as others do earlier in the play). Interrupting his monologue of darkly comic self-pity is one-hit film starlet Corinna Stroller, girlfriend of Einhorn whom he asked to drop by to say hello to Artie. She is friendly, even kindly, and stunningly attractive, but she is deaf, the result of an on-set accident involving stunt explosives. She is currently on her way to Australia to meet specialists reputed to be able to help her recover her hearing. Almost immediately three nuns appear at the apartment window (the apartment is several stories up) asking to be let in because they have been locked on the roof of the building while trying to get to a better view of the Pope and his entourage, due to go by shortly. The groupie nuns are a quirkily perfect fit in this madhouse: they have stolen binoculars from their mother superior (and lost them), are decided fans of alcoholic beverages, and hunger for snapshots of almost everything, including pictures of them hugging the television, which is airing the momentous events everyone in the room seems to be missing just outside their apartment building.

Further confusion ensues, including a melee between Ronnie and the nuns as they fight over two tickets to Yankee Stadium that Corinna has but will not be using. A military police officer arrives to arrest Ronnie, and a man in white enters to take Bananas away, but Bunny, who is pretending that she is Mrs. Arthur Shaughnessy, is taken instead. Corinna leaves to catch her flight, unwittingly toting Ronnie's gift-wrapped bomb, which explodes in the elevator. In addition to Corinna, it is revealed, two nuns have died as well. This event closes act 2, scene 1.

Scene 2 opens later that evening first with the Pope's heavily accented speech broadcast on television. The curtain rises on a set cluttered with rubble, among which Billy Einhorn has been called in to identify Corinna's body. He is devastated, having also recently lost his first wife. Billy seems to be one of the only characters in the play who experiences genuine emotions, the recently deceased Corinna being the other. Bananas, though narcotized into numbness throughout the play, does offer a poignant speech about at least being "in a place I remember feeling" (77). Guare gives his three most unlikely characters, an agent, a starlet, and a mental patient, capacity for true feeling. In contrast the callously distracted Artie is quick to tell Billy to get over his loss, the surviving nun seems to have no feelings for her deceased sisters, and Bunny prepares to seduce Billy—her new meal ticket—with her cooking. Billy snaps out of his genuineness quickly and begins to throw his authority around by calling an old acquaintance, a general, and trying to save Ronnie from incarceration. He does not realize the full extent of Ronnie's transgression, thinking him guilty only of going AWOL. Billy hopes to get Ronnie stationed in Rome while every other GI seems headed to Vietnam. Justice is certainly not served in this instance.

Then Billy falls for Bunny's food, realizes he now has an extra ticket to Australia, and offers her a job as personal assistant and cook. Stars in her eyes, Bunny accepts, and the two make their airport departure, leaving Artie and Bananas soaking up the report that all the expectant animals at the zoo are simultaneously giving birth. Abandoned by his best girl and best hope, Artie stands subdued besides Bananas, who, according to stage directions, "is serene and peaceful and beautiful in the dim light." With no sign of judgment in her voice, Bananas states, "I don't blame you for that lady, Artie. I really don't" (85).

The ending seems to be setting itself up in predictable comedic style: alone at last, the couple will have the opportunity to get to know each other, learn once again to love each other, and settle into the business of living. Bananas even gives the expected lines: "Oh God Artie, it's like we're finally alone for the first time in our life. Like it's taken us eighteen years to get from the church to the hotel room and we're finally alone. I promise you I'll be different" (86). Artie "smiles at her, hopefully," while Bananas "sits on her haunches like a little dog smiling for food," sings a song about togetherness, does several small dog tricks, and draws Artie's seemingly warm attention (86). The scene is somewhat reminiscent of the final scene in John Osborne's kitchen-sink classic *Look Back in Anger,* where husband and wife salve their wounds by playing squirrels and bears, suggesting through this lovers' game that all will be well as long as they are together. This undoubtedly is one of the elements of Osborne's play that baffled Guare: how could such a conventional ending be part of a so-called revolutionary play?

Guare, however, does not follow romantic comedy convention. Rather he has Artie do perhaps what Osborne's Jimmy Porter should have done: he and Bananas kiss, and then as "his hands go softly on her throat, she looks up at him with a beautiful smile as if she had always been waiting for this. He kisses her temples, her cheeks. His hands tighten around her throat. . . . She smiles radiantly at him. He squeezes the breath out of her throat. She falls" (86). Blue leaves drift down from above and begin to cover the apartment: "A blue spotlight appears downstage and he [Artie] steps into it. He is very happy and smiles at us" (90). Artie introduces himself as he did at the beginning of the play, this time receiving a good deal more respect—or at least more attention—than before, bathed in the blue spotlight he asked for but did not get when the play began.

Unlike Osborne's disappointingly romantic ending, Guare's ending shocks and disturbs. His farce is in many ways more realistic than Osborne's play. A hopeless idealist finally slips completely into his fantasy world, gives in to his latent insanity, and eliminates the one perceived obstruction to his surely inevitable success, destroying in the process the only person who truly loved him and perhaps could have "saved" him. It is shocking, but it is also far more memorable and perhaps also more true-to-life than the endings found in standard comic resolutions. Gene A. Plunka observes that "Guare is at his best liberating our imaginative vision through black comedy and farce, dramatic structures that work by taking the familiar and rendering it absurd, pathetic, and ultimately, terrifying."[3] Guare offers a truth that is greater than realism, doing what August Strindberg, for example, did when he expressionistically blended the psychological with the physical to create his tragic vision of the world. In Guare's case comedy is the unlikely formula that serves as the foundation for his equally complex interweaving of psychology and physicality. For him such shocks to the system have the added benefit of snapping audiences out of the numbing effects of personal complacency and taking them a step closer to a world of uncertainty, surprise, and wonder.

The House of Blue Leaves has received several major productions. It premiered at the Truck and Warehouse Theatre in New York on 10 February 1971, but in the middle of its successful run, on 3 December, the theater burned down, closing the production after 337 performances. The circumstances of the fire are themselves almost worthy of a Guare play: investigations revealed that in apparently unrelated incidents the night the theater burned, the sets and costumes were vandalized and a man was murdered in the tenement apartment next door. Despite the premature closing, the production won the New York Drama Critics' Circle Award for best American play and the Outer Critics' Circle Award, among others. The cast included Frank Converse, Harold Gould, Katherine Helmond, William Atherton, and Anne Meara. A revival was staged in 1986, directed by Jerry Zaks at Lincoln Center's Mitzi E. Newhouse Theater. It transferred to the larger-capacity Lincoln Center Broadway venue, the Vivian Beaumont Theater, where it played five months before again transferring to the Plymouth Theatre, for a total run of 398 performances. The opening night featured another stellar cast, including Swoosie Kurtz, John Mahoney, Stockard Channing, Danny Aiello, Ben Stiller, and Julie Hagerty. It won the Drama Desk

Award for outstanding revival and was nominated for a Tony Award for best play. A 2011 Broadway revival was staged at the Walter Kerr Theatre, directed by David Cromer, which opened 4 April and ran for sixteen weeks. It starred Ben Stiller, Edie Falco, and Jennifer Jason Leigh.

Reviewers of the original production were generally positive though occasionally confused, as in the case of Julius Novick, who observed that "the farce and the agony seem to violate instead of reinforce each other."[4] Henry Hewes, however, was able to work through the apparent mixed signals and other distractions to see "the American Dream of success and the destructive forces unleashed by the frustration of never achieving it."[5]

Subsequent reviews have been more appreciative. Its 1986 revival was celebrated by many, including Mel Gussow, as a work that "becomes better with time," remaining "a joyful affirmation of life—and of Mr. Guare's artistry."[6] The 2011 revival, on the other hand, seemed to go a direction Guare's work never intended. Ben Brantley opened his review: "What do you get when you take the 'sur' out of 'surrealism'? That sounds like a question in search of a punch line. But few laughs emerge from the answers provided by the somber new revival of John Guare's 'House of Blue Leaves.'" Referencing the play's history, Brantley continued that "Mr. Cromer has rebuilt his 'House' in the style of kitchen-sink dramas, the kind in which unhappy families simmer in squalor and explode with a whimper. . . . 'House' is usually described as a black comedy. Mr. Cromer's version plunges headfirst into the blackness, leaving the comedy to sink or swim."[7] In Brantley's assessment the production once again fell victim to realist theatrical preferences, for which Guare's works are rarely suited. The need to emphasize comic theatricality over realistic precision is what Guare's work requires and often what the American stage is not readily equipped to provide.

The House of Blue Leaves was not Guare's only 1971 success. That summer the New York Shakespeare Festival, at its Central Park venue, the Delacorte Theatre, produced a musical adaptation of Shakespeare's *Two Gentlemen of Verona* by Guare and director Mel Shapiro, with music by Galt McDermot (best-known for the 1967 rock musical *Hair*). In a 2011 interview, Guare explained the work's genesis, recounting Shapiro's fears as he contemplated the project: "That summer of 1971 had been a summer of great racial unrest. The summer before, they had sent *Macbeth* up to the streets around the boroughs. And when they got to 125th Street the actors were stoned—rocks were thrown at them. *Two Gentlemen* was also going to be designed for the flatbed truck, to go around the five boroughs. Mel said, if we bring these sentiments of courtly love up to the streets that are about to burst into flames, we're going to be machinegunned down."[8]

Having just worked with Guare on *House of Blue Leaves,* Shapiro asked Guare for help dealing with this quandary. The first matter they addressed was tightening the male leads' relationships: "so I wrote the song 'I Want to Be a Hot Lover,' which is a line from Shakespeare, a hot lover like the kids in the play. And 'Love's Revenge,' when Valentine falls in love, that was another phrase from Shakespeare, and that turned into a song. It was about amplifying and strengthening all the emotional connections in the play." Then, Guare reported, having cast Raúl Juliá as Proteus, Shapiro decided to include "somebody from every neighborhood we were playing. It got to be this multi-ethnic, multi-racial cast. It was a thing of such joy, and the few songs ballooned to about 32 songs" (4).

A clear product of the period, the adaptation celebrated New York City by creating a scaffold set that had the feel of city fire escapes. The cast was dressed in colorful and stylish contemporary costumes. The music had a hip, "age of Aquarius" feel to it. The production (free in Central Park) toured various venues in the city as part of its festival obligation and was a massive popular hit, free of riots and the feared machine-gunnings. After the festival run, the play moved to Broadway's St. James Theatre, again directed by Shapiro, where it ran for 614 performances, closing 20 May 1973. It won two 1972 Tony Awards, including best musical, as well as the New York Drama Critics' Circle Award for best musical, over such shows as *Grease* and *Follies*. Guare himself received the Drama Desk Award for outstanding lyrics. The cast included Juliá and Clifton Davis in the leads as well as Stockard Channing and Jeff Goldblum in the chorus.

The play is a loose rendering of Shakespeare's comedy that includes a duke who lusts for a profiteering war not unlike the Vietnam War raging at the time. This issue crystallizes the generational divide that invigorates the play and lends it real situational value. Guare and Shapiro also clarified or simplified such Shakespearean complications as the pains of lost love, preferring the upbeat, exuberant tempo of a summer musical filled with hope. Guare reports in his introduction to the illustrated book of the play that "my favorite review was in *Rolling Stone*. It said the score sounded like walking down a street in El Barrio with all the windows open and a different radio blaring out of each one. That is what we wanted to do."[9]

The musical exemplifies Guare's interest in total theater. His introduction to the published script highlights precisely how musicals inform his relationship with his much-loved New York City, including his belief in the city's irrepressible vitality. Guare addresses the fact that the standard American dream involves the idealized longing to move from the city to the country, especially bolstered by horrific headlines in the news about waves of metropolitan murders and even gruesome decapitations. But, he asserts, the city defies these horrors by revealing a larger vitality, generated by street musicians and the many urban rhythms that can be heard day and night. *Two Gentlemen of Verona* was meant to catch both the danger and the overriding beauty of the city. Cities may have been considered to be dying in the 1960s and 1970s, but Guare argued that the city is, "always, the place you come back to because it's the place where the possibilities are" (6).

Characteristically, what repulses Guare about great but sometimes dehumanizing concentrations of people such as New York City—and about human nature in general—simultaneously attracts him. Alongside opportunity, hope, optimism, and resilience run the counterparts of missed opportunity, despair, and resignation. For Guare those two rails, running side by side, are what make up the human condition.

CHAPTER 4

After *Blue Leaves*

Flush with the concurrent 1971 successes of *The House of Blue Leaves* and *Two Gentlemen of Verona,* Guare presented his next work, *Marco Polo Sings a Solo,* in July 1973 for a six-week run at the Nantucket Stage Company in Massachusetts, again directed by Mel Shapiro and featuring Piper Laurie, Beeson Carroll, and Kevin O'Connor. The play later underwent numerous revisions and had its first major production by Joseph Papp for the New York Shakespeare Festival, opening 6 February 1977 at the Public Theatre, again directed by Shapiro. The cast included Madeline Kahn, Chris Sarandon, Sigourney Weaver, and Joel Grey, all experienced to one degree or another with cabaret performance and thus suited well to Guare's theater.

Marco Polo Sings a Solo works as an interesting counterpoint to *House of Blue Leaves.* The earlier play can be seen as a study of the ways environment limits dreams. The cluttered, claustrophobic, zoolike conditions prevent the characters from fulfilling dreams and in the end lead to catastrophe. Further, the dreams these people have are not really worth having. *Marco Polo Sings a Solo* is set on a brilliantly white iceberg under an endless, clear blue sky. It is a pristine, unpolluted environment that welcomes all possibilities, free of stifling clutter or restricted vision. Trouble lurks beneath this boundless landscape of opportunity, however, given that this seemingly rock-solid foundation is actually ice floating aimlessly on the sea. Superficially, however, all things are possible. As a metaphor the play's set speaks of the unsupported and unsupportable dreamscape that is so much part of the American imagination. To this set Guare adds a cast of very successful individuals—Nobel Prize winners, movie stars, and astronauts—movers and shakers of a world on the edge of a new millennium (the play is set in 1999). Guare builds on *House of Blue Leaves,* which presented pathetic characters occupying the edges of the Western world, by depicting the icons and architects occupying the center of that world. He thereby extends his point about the futility of the American dream, demonstrating that even those who live the dream find themselves on uncertain footing.

The play centers around Stony McBride, a famous film director, whose current project, about Marco Polo's return from his thirteenth-century adventures in the Far East, is the reason for the iceberg setting: it is being shot on the iceberg's bleached white landscape off the coast of Norway. Other characters include Frank Schaeffer, an astronaut whose extraterrestrial heroics are closely watched by millions and inspire the world; Diane, Stony's wife, a formerly famous piano prodigy; and Tom Wintermouth, with whom Diane is having an affair. Tom is a Nobel Prize-winner who has secured peace in the Middle East as well as discovered a cure for cancer. Tom is called upon to take over as U.S. president in light of unforeseen events in the nation's capital. Freydis the maid is Schaeffer's wife in disguise, hiding from the celebrity event of the year, which is for her and her husband to give birth to the first millennial—in the White House. Lusty McBride, Stony's father, is a sixty-something former matinee film idol, a closeted homosexual currently working on a comeback in his son's film. Stony's mother, meanwhile, has undergone a sex-change operation in order to be a man her beloved Lusty would desire.

In this futuristic world beset by cataclysms of all sorts—Hawaii is submerged, Italy's boot has fallen off, New Zealand is bombing Canada, and the Gulf Stream has shifted and is warming Norway—everyone is obsessed with something other than the present moment, unfulfilled by today, and always looking for tomorrow. Unlike many people, however, this cast of characters' dreams of the future are not impeded by the desire for money and fame, the two things many believe to be the cornerstones of happiness. By most standards these characters have it all.

Marco Polo Sings a Solo is somewhat reminiscent of Thornton Wilder's *The Skin of Our Teeth* (1942) in its nonnaturalist style and determination to address major questions of human existence in an almost whimsical manner. In an author's note to the published version of *Marco Polo,* Guare observes that "the play is a high comedy, played very grandly and confidently as if it were some 21st century reworking of *The Philadelphia Story* with all kinds of Katherine Hepburns and Cary Grants littering the stage."[1] Though its subject matter is serious, the play refuses to be so. Critics correctly noted its lack of structure, but it is not altogether certain that this is a negative quality. The monologues in Guare's work tend to ramble, and the individual dilemmas do not entirely cohere. If one considers his central theme, however, namely that humanity is determined to live or die as a species of autonomous individuals, then it is fitting that his characters sing their solos unfettered by any real concern for anything other than themselves. The fear of failure of the characters in *Marco Polo* is brought into relief by their current high perches, as well as the fact that they are on the set of a movie celebrating the accomplishments of the great and adventurous Marco Polo.

Marco Polo's is the kind of solo effort that Frank Schaeffer undertakes in space, discovering a green planet that bears hope as the new breadbasket for an increasingly overcrowded and desperate humanity. Perhaps as significant, Wintermouth has succeeded at eliminating the biblical threat of apocalypse by negotiating the creation of the Middle Eastern state of Saudi-Israel. His other world-changing discovery is—or would have been—his cure for cancer, though in one of several disturbances onstage, the cure is lost. Stony McBride is a biological first, a child conceived by and born to a single parent, a sign of the power of science amid the waning influence of institutions such as family.

Guare's note to the play succinctly describes his ensemble: "The people want the most, need the most, have to have the best, have the most, and in their own way, are the best of their time. The problem is they know it and congratulate themselves on it a lot" (4). Bolts from heaven variously bombard the stage in a vain effort to wake up these last great hopes of humanity. However, socialized as Americans to go it alone, they no longer seem capable of doing anything new or revolutionary—certainly nothing requiring collaboration—even if they do wake up from their current self-congratulatory ego trips. They do have great potential, as their pasts verify, but Guare sees the need "to wake these people up," and through that awakening he wants "to restore nature to some kind of balance before this new century comes into being" (4). These talented people need to move away from self-congratulations and feeding only their egos. They need to reach beyond their own glory and risk applying their talents to helping less fortunate fellow humans.

Of this bunch of searching luminaries, Guare reports that only Stony "makes it. The others are too frightened to let go of themselves ultimately, in spite of the massacres and demolition. If they stopped listening to their solo, they might die" (4). Death always haunts real risk, of course, and it is that ultimate fear that immobilizes them, revealing them to be anything but the real heroes they pretend to be. Stony is the only one willing to try, and the effort is rewarded with hope.

Stony begins much like all the rest, determined to stoke the fires of his ego. In his case he believes if he completes his film, he will make Marco Polo the beacon of hope that humanity needs while at the same time making his own mark on the world. The problem is that Marco Polo, as envisioned by Stony, is anything but a model for modernity to emulate. Early in the play, however,

Stony does not realize this, given that society in general has placed Polo on a pedestal that celebrates individual accomplishment. At the same time, Stony also wishes to maintain family unity. The other ego-ridden characters show no interest in such unity, which marks Stony as unique. His transformation, however, is far from immediate and apparently requires perspective, which Guare gives him by shooting him into space in his own self-contained suit and having him enter an orbit over Frank's recently discovered alien green planet. Stony self-fertilizes the planet's plants, which creates masses of duplicate Stonys: "This is the world I want! A world populated by only me" (42). It may appear to be a dream come true, but this fantasy goes horribly dystopic virtually at the outset: "I hear a scream. One me hits another me. Is that a rape? One of the mes rapes another me? More mes now march out of more petals. . . . Each me screaming to be heard. Me! Me! Each me ignoring the other me. Each one moaning and whining Me! This is not the me I planned to be. I came up here to find Frank Schaeffer. My true self. My true father. My true son. All I see here are these mes" (42–43). Disgusted with this personal second coming of humanity, Stony incinerates the green world (which was intended to be cultivated so that it could feed Earth's inhabitants), and in a flash he returns to Earth, edified by his trek into space.

Frank, too, experiences dystopia during his visit to the planet and tries to destroy it but realizes that it persists in much the same way that ego itself is virtually impossible to subdue. He muses, "Why is it that all the things that should hold us together, help change us—love, creativity, sex, talent, dreams—those are the very elements that drive us apart and the things that you think would separate us—hate, fear, meanness—those are the very things that bind us together and keep us from growing. Keep us from changing." He wonders, "Should I go back into space and become a hero or stay here and try to win Skippy [his wife] back? The world on one hand. Me on the other. The world. Me. The world. Me" (44). He walks offstage, befuddled. As the play draws near its end, Frank reenters, dressed as a Norwegian peasant, apparently determined to win back Skippy, who has likewise gone native. So maybe Frank shows hope as well.

Skippy has not gone native for random reasons, however. Earlier in the play, several characters go into town to see a production of Henrik Ibsen's *A Doll's House* performed on trampolines. While Ibsen's Nora famously runs from domesticity by walking out of her home and into the great unknown, Skippy instead takes on a disguise and escapes *into* domestic servitude for basically the same reason: to run away from the suffocating destiny of fame that otherwise awaits her. It is an odd kind of connection that Guare is making, but a significant one. Nora's action in *A Doll's House* has been called the move that ushered in modern theater. Perhaps Guare's design was to usher in yet another epoch with plays such as *Marco Polo Sings a Solo,* moving away from individual acts of self-satisfaction and working toward a culture willing to honor service and sacrifice instead. Just this sort of turn is hinted at when Stony gives a speech that reorients Nora's action: "So when Nora left she found herself not in the outside world, but in another, a newer, a stranger room" (27). She was still trapped. The strategy of individual defiance results simply "in a newer room still damp from construction" (27). Nora's defiant and romantic gesture of running away offers little hope of positive change, because escape is not really an option. Change requires transformation and cooperation rather than isolation.

Marco Polo Sings a Solo presents the case that, because of declarations of independence by the likes of Nora, "I" continues to prevail over "us." Stony sees the error of this ego-sustaining behavior and frets over future prospects. Says Stony in the play's spotlighted final speech: "I looked at all these people waiting for a future that would never come and when it did come, when the new century finally did arrive, they would wait another hundred for yet another new century and then a hundred years for another waiting waiting waiting always for rebirth" (50–51). Finally his closing words spoken to the audience address the need for the here and now: "I realized what I had to do. . . . Descend to earth. Remove my helmet. Draw the curtain. Say Goodbye forever. Take my son. Go out into the now. Out there where you live. Into the present. Out there where you are. Grow. Change. My plant nature. Our plant nature. I celebrate that" (50).

Despite clear allusions to Christ and the Second Coming ("Should I reveal myself to them?" [51]), the revolution is far less spectacular than perhaps one would hope for but far more sustaining than could be expected from other alternatives. Guare's proffered paradigm shift apparently is to rethink human nature's plantlike dimensions. Says Stony earlier in the play, "One of the great fallacies of science is aligning man with the mammals. . . . Man is a plant. We may look like meat, but we're not meat. We can never escape. We can never change. We are planted firmly in the ground. We are what we grow out of. My plant nature" (17).

Guare asserts the delusional nature of an unfettered humankind free to roam as it chooses. Rather than dreaming of finding some utopia on a distant shore, and rather than passively waiting for an apocalyptic change to occur in a far-future millennium, people should accept who, what, and where they are as present beings "planted firmly in the ground" of their existence. They should build on that key realization. To think otherwise is to sow destruction on the order of the Shaughnessy household in *The House of Blue Leaves*, magnified by the millions who are sold on the dream of escape to either a better place or a better tomorrow.

With *Marco Polo Sings a Solo,* Guare had crafted another unusual work for the stage, and its critical reception was not kind. Peter Marks perhaps sums up the general response best: "The story, clearly, has none of the nursery-rhyme simplicity that its title suggests. Everyone on this unseasonably warm berg . . . is in high dudgeon most of the time. And though it's a busy play—Mozart, Ibsen, a cure for cancer, Fillmore East, Leif Ericsson and the musical "Hair" all figure in the very long monologues Guare generously doles out to the actors —nothing happens to these people that makes us want to get to know them. They're interchangeable pieces in some pretty silly word games."[2] Such responses from theater critics have not been unusual in Guare's career.

Rich and Famous (1974) is not as technically ambitious as *Marco Polo Sings a Solo,* though it also defies straight realism by becoming, in part, a musical to complement the plot, which involves a young playwright bent on becoming a rich and famous composer of musicals. In the play's production notes, Guare indicates that "the show is designed as a performance piece. Let us hear the songs from the play during the scene shifts of the play. Keep it bright and brilliantly high-spirited so the audience won't know where to look next. The play is about the theatre; keep it theatrical."[3] Music, song, and dance fill the stage at every turn, though it is by no means true Broadway-caliber fare.

Rich and Famous was produced in April 1974 by William Gardner at the Academy Festival Theater in Lake Forest, Illinois, directed by Shapiro and starring Ron Leibman, Linda Lavin, Charles Kimbrough, and William Jay. It transferred to the Williamstown Theater Festival the same month. In 1976 it was revised and produced by the New York Shakespeare Festival in February, directed again by Shapiro and featuring Leibman, Anita Gillette, and William Atherton.

In *Rich and Famous* Guare returns to the theme of self-entrapment by one's dreams and the attendant fear of failure and humiliation. The main character, Bing Ringling, is a young playwright hungry for fame and determined to outdistance Shakespeare, Anton Chekhov, and all the rest by writing a musical adaptation of Dante's *Divine Comedy* called *Spreaded Thin,* drawing on his own life as the inspiration for the character of Dante. Bing's "muse" is Leanara, whom he considers destined to rival Dante's Beatrice. Though Bing aspires to wealth and fame, forces are against him, not the least of which is that he is not very talented. Furthermore his producer, Veronica Culpp-Vestige, has taken on the project because she needs a failure in order for her otherwise complete career to have its one successful comeback—after all "in order to have a comeback, one must fail" (13). Veronica believes she has discovered a sure failure in Bing's "masterpiece." Dreams of success abound throughout the play. Bing symptomatically wears two sets of monogrammed cufflinks, R and F, mixing and matching them in various combinations of Rich and Famous.

When Bing's best friend from childhood, reigning cinema superstar Tybalt Dunleavy, takes interest in the lead role and threatens the project with success, Veronica turns Tybalt away. When the flop arrives, Leanara cares little about Bing's feelings since she is discovered on opening night and promptly leaves for Hollywood. Undaunted by failure, Bing and his vain, comically (or tragically) over-the-hill collaborator, Anatol Torah, are planning a musical by combining the *Iliad* and *Odyssey* into the *Odiad*. Anatol is frankly happy about the *Divine Comedy* flop because now Bing can concentrate on Homer. Matters worsen further for Bing, however, when Anatol realizes his own comeback would be better served if he could get Bing to introduce him to Tybalt.

In a world where failure is the norm, Tybalt Dunleavy has everything. He is a James Dean–like figure, in town to promote his current blockbuster hit, *Gangland,* which is receiving premiere screenings around the world. His face is on an animated Times Square billboard, which occupies the whole stage backdrop and is larger than life, flashing several times throughout the performance to remind the audience of his success. For all his fame, Tybalt is a pretty nice guy. He searches out Bing's play when he gets into town and attends the opening (and only) performance. He invites Bing to his Algonquin Hotel suite, and he seems to have the sense not to encourage Torah's advances.

Tybalt is rich and famous and also young and much beloved. Torah, on the other hand, while still clinging to (diminishing) wealth and fame, is certainly no longer young. His circumstance gives Guare the opportunity to present the desperate effects of aging in a world where youthful vitality is the ideal. Torah has discovered exclusive establishments in Germany that he calls "death bars," "where people go to kill or be killed. Depending on which side you wear your keys, on which arm you wear your mourning band" (26). The killings in these bars transfer vitality from one life source to another, vampire-like, and Torah is prepared to kill if it will preserve his youth. Upon learning that Bing knows Tybalt and will introduce them, Anatol proposes to "fly to Germany. Have a quick kill. A good death douche. Get all the death vibrations out of me. Fill myself with life. Jet back here rosy cheeked" (27). Betrayed by Anatol, who has decided that Tybalt has more youthful vitality and greater prospects than Bing, Bing leaves Anatol to his own devices.

After having written 843 unproduced plays and one flopped production, Bing returns deflated to his childhood home and his hopelessly obsessive, idol-worshiping parents. They have insisted on Bing becoming a success virtually since his conception, in hopes that his life of fame and fortune will validate their merely normal existences and sacrifices. Their worship of Bing extends to saving literally everything from his childhood, even excrement, duly bronzed. Dad reveals the effects of his obsession with fame by his uncontrolled, stream-of-consciousness spouting of famous names at any instigation. Mom speaks to Bing, while Dad drums on:

MOM: Be like the men who've tattooed their names on life.
DAD: Who've put their names in the Dictionary of Life.
MOM: The Webster's Dictionary of Life.
DAD: Noah Webster.
MOM: And such love:
DAD: Bessie Love.
MOM: We never minded if you had an Oedipal complex because Oedipus was a King.
DAD: A Dennis King. Billy Jean King. That's my girl. My Ziegfeld girl. (34)

Obsessed with having their son make a name for them—for any reason, as long as it is a memorable one—this family is extremely dysfunctional, lacking communication skills or any understanding of Bing's true needs. Finally Bing shoots his parents. They refuse to die, though, symbolizing his inability to escape their gravitational pull.

Along with this episode, Guare offers yet another "typical" domestic situation, having Bing meet his childhood sweetheart in an art gallery selling a famous painting attributed to her grandfather. Since high school Alison has married well but clearly without love. Now she spends time literally going into her own looking-glass world, jumping in and out of the frame of her grandfather's picture. The ultimate escapist, Alison observes, "You see a movie you like, don't you just walk right into it? I take out snapshots and I walk right into them. I take my car and drive into the yearbook" (30). This she does in order to survive, conceding, "I'll never be rich and famous like you are, but I can have a life" (31). It is not much of a life, however, if living in this bleak, empty version of the here and now is what one means by living.

Despondent, Bing climbs the Times Square billboard, apparently deciding to end it all by jumping. On the billboard platform, he finds Tybalt dressed in saffron robes and himself about to jump. Tybalt repeatedly apologizes for not knowing that Bing wanted to be rich and famous: "If I'd known you wanted to be R & F, I'd have given you my life" (41). Clearly he considers it a life not worth having. In fact his life is no longer even Tybalt's to give or preserve. In an act of marketing genius, his handlers have sold his death to the highest bidders, guaranteeing Tybalt will go down in history along with such forever-young icons as James Dean, Marilyn Monroe, and Jesus. Tybalt has bought into the plan: “It’ll be a multi-million dollar industry” (42). Just prior to the moment that theaters will be emptying his fans onto the streets, he confesses to Bing in a speech that could have come from *Marco Polo Sings a Solo:* “I always thought about the future, so much I never remembered the past. I wanted to be rich and famous badly. But we’re afraid to grow. I was afraid to take the plunge into immortality” (43). Marketing has now confused him into seeing a profit in taking a fatal plunge into immortality, and he does it. Once again Guare asserts the hollowness of that which Bing and others pursue. Tybalt says he loved Bing’s play but could not be part of it because “it’s not big enough. It doesn’t fit the legend” (43). In virtually every way imaginable, he is trapped by his celebrity rather than set free by it. He can do only what befits his stature, limiting him in ways that is the opposite of what is expected of fame.

In the earlier scene with his parents—as he tries to describe his Dante play—Bing seems to have begun to understand the world about him: “Purgatory is people not seeing reality for what it is. . . . Let me see life the way it is so I’ll know what to do with it. Let me see reality for what it is. Let me see things the way they are so I’ll know what I have to do” (39). Lucidity is only a temporary condition in this play, though. A big song-and-dance number closes things out, with an actress who is dressed to look “like some bizarre version of Bing” (44) singing:

> Before I was born
> Angels fluttered down
> and promised I’d be
> Rich and Famous.
> Then I got born
> To earth I sputtered down
> Now I’m not Rich
> And I’m not famous.
> Where are those angels with their broken promises?
> Do I fall in line with the other Doubting Thomases?
> Where are those angels? What do they think they’re doing?
> If they don’t show up soon, I’m suing. (44–45)

The song and Bing’s despairing final gesture summarize the tragic dilemma that Guare persistently though comically presents in his works.

Humans have been burdened with visions of great success, which unfortunately is only available to a distinct few. Moreover the list of this successful few seems rather randomly generated, belying the old adage that hard work will lead to success. The choice for each individual, ultimately, is to look at the odds and determine whether he or she is the one who will beat them or should settle into an existence without such ambitions. The path people most long to pursue, however—wealth and fame—is virtually guaranteed to dead-end in bitter disappointment. Fame and fortune destroys and entraps, failing in every measure to provide the contentment so many seek. Even if one does manage to beat the odds, such a victory typically only wins disappointment.

Nevertheless humans still generally ignore these sobering truths and run headlong into inevitable failure. *Rich and Famous* ends with the point pantomimed for the audience: "Bing very proudly and easily removes one cufflink and tosses it with great resolve in front of him. . . . Bing tries to undo the other cufflink. It won't come loose. It's a struggle. He can't give up that final cufflink. He lowers his hands in dismay" (45). Wisdom is ultimately betrayed by desire, or so seems Guare's tragic, comic message.

During this busy time, Guare brought yet another project to the stage. *Landscape of the Body* was produced in July 1977 by William Gardner at the Academy Festival Theatre, directed by John Pasquin and starring Shirley Knight and F. Murray Abraham. It transferred to the Public Theatre in New York City on 12 October 1977, presented by Joseph Papp and the New York Shakespeare Festival.

The play is framed by scenes on a ferry to Nantucket, with most of the action occurring in flashback. The ferry—something like the mythical ferry over the River Styx—is occupied by two people, one wearing a mask, another writing notes, putting them in a bottle, and throwing them overboard. It evolves that the two are Holahan, a former New York police officer, and Betty, a woman he once interrogated for the gruesome, still-unsolved murder and decapitation of her fourteen-year-old son. Holahan takes off his mask once he realizes Betty recognizes him. The flashback part of the play shifts between an interrogation room and events in the lives of the boy and his mother. Furthermore much of the play is controlled by its narrator, the ghost of Betty's sister Rosalie, a once free-living woman who died the day her sister and nephew came to New York from their Maine home looking to bring her back to her north woods family. Being dead and virtually omniscient, Rosalie is able to reveal more than any living narrator or investigator could. The audience benefits from her insights, while the onstage characters are left with questions never to be answered.

The theatrics are intriguing and actually do much to contribute to the strange world these two living characters occupy. The play takes place in a world manufactured from the memories of the living and the dead, and this idea of a memory-crafted world is central to the imaginative theatricality that Guare utilizes. For example ghostly Rosalie enters at crucial moments and makes direct contact with the audience. She works from a stage manager's perspective with deliberately stagey, Brechtian pronouncements such as "Scene.

In which Betty wishes her sister was still alive."[4] The audience is constantly reminded that it is in the theater experiencing a reconstructed past that suggestively transcends the truth of mere reality. The play presents a murder mystery of a sort, though the mystery remains only among the uninformed living who are bounded by the stage. The audience knows all, and therein lies the truly engaging dramatic tension: between audience and characters rather than between characters themselves.

In addition to the theatrical devices, the play also incorporates gritty, street-level realism. Rosalie moonlighted in porn while living—calling it the entertainment industry—and worked with a huckster in tricking well-to-do engaged couples to purchase questionable honeymoon vacations. She edged herself into the fantasy-generating and dream-making business, albeit at a low, unsavory, and even illegal end of it. These fantasies and dreams all too often prove desperate, though in Guare's work such desperation frequently turns darkly comic. Rosalie's boss, Raulito, for example, a poor Cuban raised in poverty in the Cuban hills, believed as a youth that rich and famous people always wore eveningwear. This psychologically implanted impression never leaves him and stimulates him to dress in kind whenever he can, even though he now knows the truth. Rosalie and Raulito have joined the game of buying their dreams by selling fake dreams in the form of honeymoons to others.

Meanwhile Betty and her son, Bert, travel down from Bangor in an attempt to bring Rosalie home to her family. She refuses to return and tries to tempt Betty to stay instead, but Rosalie is killed by a speeding (and unrepentant) cyclist before anything is settled. Betty curiously responds by stepping into Rosalie's life, even completing the porn films her sister had begun and continuing the same relationship Rosalie had with Raulito. Bert finds friends in the city, and he and friend Donny devise their own foolproof profit-making scheme whereby Bert lures pedophiles into their apartment with promises of sex for pay. Donny bludgeons them with a monkey wrench, and they steal watches and wallets, toss the victims into the hallway, and have cops take them away under the presumption that they are drunks or junkies.

The complex scheme that Bert and Donny have developed was spawned by an episode in real life that struck Guare's fancy and in turn led to the whole play. He summarizes: "I had seen kids like these in a booth at a coffee shop on Hudson Street, the boys' arms filled with wristwatches, black, gold, silver, whispering delightedly to the girls, who kept snapping at the bands, dials, faces. Where had the boys got these watches? I mean they had a *lot* of watches. I went home and wrote out what I thought they might be saying."[5] Guare folded imagination into his reality-inspired work and derived a theater that is distinctively his. Similarly Raulito's fate apparently has its origin in an urban legend. Bert and Donny are in a bank, and Bert writes a bank-robbery note on the back of a deposit slip: "Hand over all your money or I'll blow your brains on the wall" (152). They put the slip back into the pile of unused deposit slips, expecting a big joke for the person who fills out and presents that form. It is Raulito, walking into the bank and contributing to his Christmas Club account, who is the butt of the joke and victim of the fatal shooting that follows.

Quirkiness aside, the play is one that searches for the seeds of happiness in the form of family. The opening ferry ride begins with Holahan pointing out the compound that is the Kennedy family home and boasting that he can name all the Dionne quintuplets. In the context of the play, the idea of family seems to hold the key to relieving America's general malaise. Everyone in the play is looking for the stability of a family life, but only if it is glamorous, sensational, and unique, or at least interesting. Betty and Rosalie have family back in Bangor, but the only element of interest to the city seems to be that it is the hub of a thriving charter plane industry. One character, the now insane Durwood Peach, saw the apparent idyllic tranquility of the girls' earlier home life when he sold Good Humor ice cream sandwiches and watched the family on their front porch. He is now a family man himself in South Carolina, with a beautiful country property, lovely wife, and caring parents. He cannot help thinking of Betty, however, and has decided to drive to Maine (and then redirect himself to New York) to ask her to marry him and come with him to his Carolina home. Durwood is part of a portrait of domestic bliss, a person who seemingly has it all, but he is trapped in the culture of acquisition and is unable to find satisfaction. He describes the nature of his illness: "To pursue the unattainable. My doctor says that's my problem. . . . I won't lie to you. I have been sick. And to be cured, I must once in my life obtain the unobtainable or I will die" (133). He little understands that he is already in possession of what many consider the ideal life in the country. What one has, it appears, is irrelevant, however, because there is still the rest of the world, and even that is not enough.

Raulito puts it most succinctly when he describes his impoverished childhood in Cuba and how his dreams were cultivated by what little of the free-market world he had access to: "Occasionally a magazine would appear in our village and I'd see pictures of evening gowns and spangles and barrettes in the hair and these high heels. I thought that was rich people. I thought if you were rich and lived in the city or lived in America that was what the average American family hung around in. . . . The dreams we have as kids, they're the dreams we never get over" (122). They are dreams Bert has, too, collecting watches way beyond his need, merely to fill his arm and impress a girl. Perhaps for him the illusion of being able to take control of something as fundamental as time is what he thinks he needs for security.

It seems that family alone may not be enough. It is not enough for Durwood, and it does not seem to be enough for Bert (or for Betty and Rosalie, for that matter), though Bert's family comprises only a single mother. Love does seem to exist in this small family unit nevertheless. Perhaps the most poignant episode in the play is between Bert and Betty, at home with Bert washing Betty's hair and the two of them talking. The topics may not be conventional fare between mother and son, but the bonding is genuine and the love apparent. There is something sensible to Betty's decision to take Durwood up on his offer of marriage, considering the more secure, healthier world that the former Good Humor man could provide. Her current situation in New York as sister substitute, after all, is far from ideal. But her decision to go with Durwood and leave Bert on his own—though only temporarily—is the decision that leads to her son's death.

After Betty leaves with Durwood, Bert has a brief moment of panic that his mother may not return. The panic attack frightens Donny, who—experienced in the matter of silencing people—cudgels Bert with his stock-in-trade monkey wrench to silence him. In an instant he is dead. The ensuing question is what to do with Bert's body. The decision to decapitate him is made by another of Bert's friends, and still another is involved before all is over. The gruesome part is that these teenagers are already numbed to reality and see this as only another part of the sensational world that they are about to inherit. Their secret will go with them to the grave, it appears. The audience, however, benefits from its ghostly guide's special knowledge: all of this reenactment happens compliments of Rosalie's posthumous point of view. The who, what, and why of Bert's murder remains a mystery to the on-stage characters, however.

Betty returns to New York after she discovers Durwood's mental instability, her dream of security dashed when she meets his kindly parents and wife in South Carolina. The horrors of her son's murder greet her. In the end Betty, once a prime suspect in the unsolved murder, and Holahan, the lead investigator now dismissed from the force, ride the ferry beyond the Kennedy compound and quite possibly into a new life together. Meanwhile Rosalie reveals what she and Betty were talking about on the porch the day Betty captured Durwood's fancy. She was describing the world as a place humanity hovered over in free flight, tempted by hooks that would drag them down if they were caught. In a speech somewhat reminiscent of *Marco Polo Sings a Solo,* Rosalie tells Betty to "wait for that one day we can bite free and get back out there in space where we belong, sail back over water over skies, into space . . . never to return hurrah to earth and we'll look back and can't even see these lives here anymore" (166). The speech is also reminiscent of the final act of Thornton Wilder's *Our Town,* which is filled with commentary from beyond the grave on the grander perspective that includes life and living but does not obsess over it. In *Landscape of the Body,* it is the abstraction of a young woman repeated after she has prematurely died, spoken by her ghost from the pedestal of afterlife. Curiously Guare includes an epigraph from a Wallace Stevens poem, "Esthétique du Mal," at the end of the play's printed text: "The greatest poverty is not to live/In a physical world, to feel that one's desire/Is too difficult to tell from despair" (167). Escape is not the answer to life's ills and evils, though the alternative is not easy to envision, much less to pursue.

Perhaps in the end, it might be that the ferry trip Betty and Holahan are taking may in fact be a metaphoric trip across the River Styx. Instead of traveling from the land of the living to the land of the dead, however, the trip may be headed in the other direction. If so the play offers a degree of hopefulness amid grim reality.

Writing of the 2006 Signature Theater Company revival of *Landscape of the Body,* Ben Brantley reports, "There is something almost tragic in this mythology of aspiration, since everyone is ultimately locked in isolation not only from the Good Life but also from one another. Yet the forms of longing in 'Landscape' are endearingly plucky, even jaunty."[6] Comedy finds a way into even a dark and despairing work such as *Landscape of the Body.*

Bosoms and Neglect addresses a similar elemental despair and the same urge for family found in *Landscape of the Body,* but in the case of this 1979 play, the sensationalism is muted and theatricality reduced to more-or-less realistic levels. The play opened 3 May 1979 at the Longacre Theatre in New York City, again directed by Shapiro, following an initial engagement at the Goodman Theatre in Chicago.

To much the same degree that *The House of Blue Leaves* portrayed an elemental fear of personal humiliation, *Bosoms and Neglect* tackles the same subject through its study of slow death in a world of benign neglect. The three-character play opens in the apartment of a blind, elderly, rather unstable woman with a man at the door, Scooper, saying that he has found a doctor that makes house calls. The woman complains about losing her bladder and spending nights behind the curtains of an open window with a crucifix and a Kotex praying to Saint Jude, patron saint of lost causes, to cure an open chest sore. This ritual has gone on, apparently, for two years, about the last time Scooper visited his mom. The relationship is strained, with Scooper implying Henny, the elderly woman, is or has been insane. This scene, labeled "Prologue," ends just before the doctor enters, with Scooper's reacting to what must be a hideous open sore on one of her breasts.

Act 1 proper opens a few days later with Scooper in the apartment of Deirdre, a woman who goes to the same psychoanalyst that Scooper uses. It took several years of indecision on Scooper's part, passing in the waiting room and perhaps even engaging in a bit of stalking, before he actually initiated a conversation with Deirdre. Both people are in their elements talking about psychiatric treatments and bemoaning the fact that their doctor is about to take a month-long vacation, leaving these highly dependent patients to fend for themselves. Scooper discusses his mom's impending mastectomy, personally suspecting that she planned it all in order to disrupt his plans to run away with his best friend's wife, which was to happen later the same afternoon. Deirdre talks about once being a nun, about an abusive husband, and about the death of her parents in a car crash years ago. They learn that they share a fierce addiction to reading. Deirdre's apartment, in fact, is cluttered with well-bound, high-quality books, most of which both of them seem to have read. Later it is revealed that Deirdre's father is actually alive and is a former mafioso who was turned in by his daughter and now no longer speaks to her. This matter of generational noncommunication is an extension of the central problem between Scooper and his mother. Scooper admits their relationship is poor because he simply does not know her, in large measure because their family life was less than ideal: Scooper's parents married late, and his father was emotionally distant.

Both Deirdre and Scooper are comforted by books and consoled by their analyst. Neither seems capable of meaningful relationships. Both expand on the problem of neglect, discussing a certain class of neglected books but also acknowledging general neglect among humans and the world at large. Neglect and disregard extend to current affairs as well. Scooper's affair with his best friend's wife will shortly come to an end, and he loses the friend as well, who is also his job partner. Deirdre brings everything to a head by observing, "We both share a guilt about the way we neglected a parent" (212). Neglect of potentially nurturing relationships is a general condition. Now the two uncomfortably joust back and forth in different states of emotion, sometimes warm and vulnerable, other times distant and aggressive, each trying to connect but without the sufficient experience to succeed. Scooper finally concludes: "We're subsidiary characters in everybody's lives. That's the . . . joke of our lives. We spend all our time babbling to Herr Doktor across the street about ourselves and we don't figure in anyone's life. I bring my life to Dr. James and we turn my life into a lullaby until I'm as fictional to myself as any one of these books are to me."[7] This meeting between two socially inept but not unattractive people ends with Scooper in a rage trying to destroy Deirdre's apartment. The result is a melee in which they stab each other with paper knives, leaving each exhausted and baffled by the outburst of emotive energy they both experienced and witnessed.

Act 2 opens in Henny's hospital recovery room, with Scooper entering in a wheelchair, himself recovering from the wounds he got in Deirdre's apartment. Henny, being blind, does not realize Scooper is actually a patient until much later, and Scooper does nothing to reveal the truth even as he charges his mother with having spent a lifetime lying to him about almost everything. About Henny's surgery, he reports, "they said for all the neglect, you had the body of a fifty-two year old woman" (223). Scooper means neglect in a physical sense, but neglect in virtually all its forms has been present in Scooper and Henny's relationship.

The breast cancer strikes deeply into Henny's consciousness. She hates the word *breast,* preferring *bosom,* and tells Scooper that it is the part of her body she was most proud of. Now all she has is memories. The same with Scooper, who recalls they were his earliest source of nourishment. The conversation extends to Henny's complaints about Scooper's obsession with books that nobody else reads; Henny's suicide attempts (intentional or accidental) and her premarried, married, and postmarried life; Scooper's problems with women and with making and keeping friends in general; and Henny's hope that Scooper was gay rather than mentally ill. Scooper's juvenile nickname was his idea; Henny insists he take his real name, a grown-up name, and grow up in the process. Among all the tales and anecdotes, Henny most poignantly recalls the middle-age period of her life when she finally got married (I was "a forty-two-year-old virgin" [228]). Scooper in turn talks to his mother about the event that finally led to his dependency on his therapist: "Your son followed a young girl for five blocks because he knew she would be kidnapped and he had to protect her from the aliens who would kill her" (233). He "pulled this girl into a side-street to let her know she was protected" (233). Scooper eventually found his way to a psychiatric ward. What is particularly curious about this episode in his life is that he came to believe that the woman he accosted might actually have been the proverbial girl of his dreams: "I said for years I look for the perfect girl. One day I snap. . . . What do I do? I mug Miss Right" (234). Scooper goes through this confessional and wants to know more about his mother because "I'm trying to clear my life out. I don't want to be crazy like you" (234).

Through all the detail, the play winds down on several qualified but positive notes. First Deirdre is also in the hospital recovering from wounds. She says her father has put a contract out on Scooper for assaulting his daughter, but eventually she confesses her dad is not part of the Mafia after all. The two discuss neglected authors, emphasizing the word *neglect* throughout the dialogue.

Eventually it becomes evident that this woman, another victim of a Scooper assault, is this time Miss Right, and the two leave the stage with apparent dreams of a better future.

Scooper is not present when Henny reawakens and tells a tale of an event when he was an infant. It echoes a recurrent dream that Scooper has suffered through most of his adult life. It involves his mother using him as an infant to cudgel the man she loved, who had neglected her and thereby led her to accept an unhappy alternative man to marry. She does not realize that she is speaking to no one—Scooper is gone—when she notes that his life *may* be taking a turn for the better. Henny tells Scooper in absentia that shortly after the run-in with that love of her life, Henny says she "sat by your [Scooper's] bed. Stared and stared at you. This was my prayer. A better life for you. You woke up. You looked at me. I wanted that for you" (248). Not knowing how to provide a better life for Scooper has resulted in decades of guilt-ridden neglect on Henny's part, and now she is slipping back into a world of neglect herself. Perhaps, however, the play suggests, Scooper and Deirdre will create a relationship not diseased by neglect.

Reviewing the 1986 Perry Street Theatre revival, Mel Gussow admiringly observed the play's overall effect: "The diagnosis, as before, is a case of theatrical schizophrenia. The work still seems like two disparate one-act dialogues sewn together to make up a full-length play. However, for all its structural weakness, 'Bosoms and Neglect' is more interesting than many other current plays and its second act—a mother-and-son confrontation—arouses one's compassion."[8] Though Guare may not have satisfied some critics' structural expectations with this work—or with many others—to some the continuing union of disparate elements on multiple levels is what makes his work so engaging.

In 1981 Guare's one-act *In Fireworks Lie Secret Codes* was produced by the Lincoln Center Theater Company as part of its one-act play festival. It returns to a world of American successes, with five characters (simply identified as #1, #2, etc.) watching July 4 fireworks from the expansive terrace of a penthouse apartment on the West Side of Manhattan, overlooking the Hudson River. The play has a rhythm to it guided by the punctuation of fireworks that leads the characters to repeat one-line comments and exclamations as they jolt out of the conversations that precede each firework eruption. One character, #4 (a woman), is frightened someone will fall from the balcony, leading the audience perhaps to feel that the play will suffer a catastrophic ending, but the event never comes to pass. The characters, though presumably best friends, enter into isolated monologues about their pasts that receive little comment from the others. One compares Macy's to Bloomingdale's, another recalls a past Christmas in the Holy Land, and yet another declares a need to return home to

Britain. One rare moment of interaction involves two of the characters helping to recount an anecdote about a subway encounter told by a third character. Character #2, the woman homesick for Britain, recounts the time she visited New Orleans, reflecting, "I always thought Tennessee Williams was a poet. He just wrote down the way people spoke."[9] She adds to the point something that she discovered while riding a bus in London: "I always thought of that line as the Harold Pinter bus line. That's all poetry is. Pinter understood the neighborhood on an ordinary day. A day that's not a holiday. The lingo of the streets. The way the rhythm of the town fits on the tongue. On an ordinary day. Not an hysterical day like a holiday. No poetry on holidays" (13). Guare asserts that the mundane and ordinary is the poetry of life, not elevated verse celebrating elevated occasions. In this short play he creates comfortable but hollow characters, not even worthy of names, and props them up by showing them in their holiday finery, orchestrated rather unnaturally into a rhythm by the fireworks, though a rhythm they are unlikely to find otherwise in their daily lives. It is a short play, but it describes Guare's interest in how a mundane reality elevates to the poetic when it is accurately absorbed and presented.

CHAPTER 5

Atlantic City (1980)

Atlantic City, Guare's best-known cinematic effort (released in 1980), is a collaboration between the playwright and filmmaker Louis Malle, who admired Guare's work—particularly *Landscape of the Body,* which he saw in 1977 at the Public Theater in New York—and asked him to consider working on a film project. Malle had secured funds from Canadian producers for his next project, and the producers were anxious to take advantage of a Canadian tax break that required the film to be completed by the end of 1979. The film has little to do with Canada except that three of the main characters are from Moose Jaw, Saskatchewan. Even so, the film's premise hinges on the fact that all three characters desperately want to leave Canada.

Despite not winning an Academy Award, *Atlantic City* has the distinction of being among only forty-one films in the history of the Oscar to be nominated for all of the "big five" awards: best picture, best director for Malle, best actor for Burt Lancaster, best actress for Susan Sarandon, and best original screenplay for Guare. It did, however, win the Golden Lion Award at the Venice Film Festival in 1980 in a tie with John Cassavetes's *Gloria.* Malle contacted Guare in July 1979, and the collaboration began in earnest when Guare took Malle to New Jersey to see the demolition and reconstruction projects being undertaken in Atlantic City. The city's transformation turned out to be a perfect prevailing metaphor for urban death and rebirth, a motif that interested both men. Quickly agreeing to pursue a project set in Atlantic City, Guare created a list of characters inspired from that single visit: Sally Matthews, a woman fleeing the tedium of her native Canada, currently working at an oyster bar and taking classes in order to become a blackjack dealer and someday moving to Monaco; Sally's estranged hometown husband, Dave, a smooth-talking petty thief living with Sally's dreamy, pregnant Hare Krishna sister,

Chrissy. Residents of Atlantic City include a middle-aged, bedridden woman, Grace, whose past includes marriage to a mobster (since killed) and dreams of winning Betty Grable lookalike contests; and her much-abused, meticulously well-dressed manservant and sexual partner, Lou Pasco, who lives off the paltry pay he receives from her and from a minor numbers racket he runs. Lou claims to have once been a member of a Mafia-style gang, but he is now a shadow of this past self. He insists on using his income to dress and groom as if he were still a man of means and importance.

Vincent Canby suggested that the film's particular strength is its pervasive mood, calling it "one of the most romantic and perverse ghost stories ever filmed, set not in a haunted castle but in a haunted city, the contemporary Atlantic City, a point of transit where the dead and the living meet briefly, sometimes even make love, and then continue on their individual ways."[1] He added of the film's location: "It's a place of myth, of legends and dreams, most of them pretty tacky. It's beautiful and squalid and, like the movie itself, sometimes rueful and sometimes funny." Memorably idiosyncratic, *Atlantic City* has the definite feel of a work by Guare, including in its highly ambiguous "moral."

Sally is played by Susan Sarandon, and Lou by Burt Lancaster. The supporting cast includes Kate Reid as Grace, Robert Joy as Dave, and Hollis McLaren as Chrissy. The film opens on a Philadelphia street corner where a cocaine drop is about to take place. The drop location is a phone booth, where Dave slips in and steals the stash before it can be retrieved by its intended recipients. He and pregnant Chrissy hitchhike their way to Atlantic City, planning to stay with Sally, Chrissy's sister and Dave's estranged wife, while Dave sells his ill-gotten gains. Sally is introduced listening to opera music on a cassette player—part of a self-improvement program—and applying lemon oil over her arms and breasts to eliminate the smell of the oyster bar she works at by day. She is viewed by an aroused Lou from behind a curtained window in his apartment across an alley. This opening sequence succinctly describes the main characters. Dave is a parasitic, amoral opportunist; Chrissy is spacy and unaware of what is happening around her; Sally is quietly ambitious and unaware of her sexual appeal; and Lou is an aging fantasist longing well past his prime for a "return" to a life of fulfillment he never actually experienced.

When the two vagabonds arrive, Sally, morally outraged and personally wounded by the betrayals of her husband and sister, initially refuses to help. Pragmatism prevails, however, and Sally eventually agrees to put them up in large part out of concern for her dreamy flower child of a sister. Dave leaves them to meet with a local dealer at a sleazy bar, where he and his stash are met with suspicion by the regulars. He is given directions to a running poker game in a dilapidated hotel room, but before he leaves the bar, he bumps into Lou, who recognizes Dave as someone Sally knows. Dave quickly sees an opportunity to charm the old man and convinces Lou to let him use Lou's apartment to cut the drugs. He then talks the well-groomed older man into dealing the drugs to the gamblers (since Dave is dressed less presentably) for a cut in the profits. The mob bosses in Philadelphia who lost their drugs hear that a new dealer is selling high-quality cocaine in Atlantic City, however, and they make the obvious connection. Dave is tracked down and brutally knifed at the end of a chase scene around the scaffolding of an elevator car park.

Since there is no way for the mobsters to make a connection between Dave and Lou, the older man inherits the drugs and the money with no strings attached. Seizing the opportunity and without much real consideration, Lou buys flashy new clothes for himself and for another hapless old buddy also down on his luck. He also meets up with Sally, awkwardly befriends her, and paternally offers to pay for her dead husband's funeral. After all, these ill-gotten gains by thieves' logic probably really belong to her, though Lou chooses not to reveal the source of his largesse or his brief acquaintance with Dave. For Sally Lou's outlook on the world is wise—he is a good talker—and his demeanor worldly. She sees an opportunity for further self-improvement by having him teach her about the ways of the world. As she is drawn to Lou, she moves away from the protection of another stylish older man, her blackjack teacher, whose designs on her appear to be less than fatherly or noble. Lou is something of an anachronism in this crumbling Atlantic City of drugs, prostitution, and gambling. He seems to have heart in a world suitable only for heartless hustling.

For the moment, at least, Lou is living the good life, and Sally seems happy for the first time in a long while, until the mobsters track her down, identifying her as Dave's wife and likely aware of where the drugs are hidden. They ransack her apartment and slap her around in the petrified presence of Lou. Lou, it turns out, is a coward, a man of false bravado who would panic and run in his early days in the mob. He cut out on Grace's husband and Lou's boss as he was gunned down. This information in part explains Grace and Lou's curiously interdependent relationship.

An interesting subplot in the film involves the gaudy, tacky, bedridden Grace. To keep Chrissy occupied while making his rounds, Dave brings her to Grace's apartment, and she begins a course of physical therapy for the older woman, who resists until she experiences positive effects. The two eventually become friends, with Grace's maternal instincts kicking in and transforming her into a kinder person. The movie suggests that events will work out well for these two lost souls.

Lou's happy ending, however, is far from certain. Traumatized by the sight of violence, he returns to the poker party and sells more of his stash, packs his bags, and heads to the bus station, apparently fleeing Atlantic City and headed to Florida. Sally, fired from the casino when it becomes known that her murdered husband was a hood, follows Lou and corners him at the station. The two mobsters arrive in turn and begin to rough Sally up again, again humiliating Lou in the process. This time, however, Lou pulls out a pistol and guns down the two thugs.

He and Sally take the mobsters' Cadillac and flee the city. Lou is ecstatic, having reclaimed his manhood and redeemed his life with his act of courage, and Sally, now wise to the money Lou has, begins to dream big about her future. They hole up in a roadside motel, watching the news reports of the Atlantic City gangland murder. Lou cannot resist taking the phone into the bathroom, secretively calling Grace, and boasting about his actions. As he returns from the bathroom, he sees Sally splitting the money and apparently preparing to leave. Lou enters, self-controlled, and talks about breakfast. They decide on pizza. He gives her the keys to the car, pretending not to know her intentions. She looks longingly at him and tells him that he saved her life as she leaves to find her future.

Lou returns to Atlantic City and to Grace, who has new respect for him, and they walk the boardwalk arm in arm. Chrissy, who was born to land on her feet, has found a temporary home with Grace, who takes the younger woman in as mother to daughter. Chrissy and her child will be just fine whatever may come.

Like Guare's work for the stage, *Atlantic City* is less concerned with conventional approaches to morality than with confronting the complexities of competing codes and beliefs in a world unsuited for conventional ways of thinking. Dave's gruesome murder is horrible, but he is a smooth-talking parasite who brings it on himself. His death serves the dramatic purpose of emphasizing the evil of the two mobsters responsible for it. Their deaths in turn almost literally breathe new life into Lou, a man desperate to live with a dignity that has so far escaped him. The murder in defense of a woman's honor seems justified. The money that drives the film's plot comes from stolen drugs, but those ill-gotten profits change the lives of two sympathetic and fundamentally good characters. Nothing is clean in this movie, but Sally and Lou manage to escape the film's seaminess, drawing rebirth and regeneration out of Atlantic City's sordid decay.

This case study of situational ethics is typical of Guare. It is not necessarily a case of upholding some particular philosophy of relativism as it is a matter of demonstrating that relativism exists, for better and for worse. Guare makes this and similar points throughout his work. Does a good-hearted but misguided bomber deserve to escape the law? Do abused and misused youths deserve a second chance though involved in murder and mutilation? Should Lou go to jail for killing two mobsters? Though these questions periodically arise in Guare's work, they are not the kind of questions that truly concern him. People in such circumstances do escape justice with frightening frequency. That is not Guare's point either, however. Rather in a world where law and order only succeed to a certain point, the more important question is how to survive. Is there a natural justice to existence that transcends the petty, ultimately inconsequential efforts of human-generated justice? Probably not, if one goes by the lessons learned in Guare's theater. His plays survey a darker terrain than that of police stations and courtrooms. The same terrain is effectively studied in *Atlantic City.*

CHAPTER 6

Capturing America's Heritage

The idea of the loss of the American dream would be central to even the briefest summary of the themes of John Guare's theater. According to Guare the American ideals of life, liberty, and the pursuit of happiness, which represent so much good to humanity, somewhere went off track. Or perhaps the dream was never quite as firmly rooted in virtue as Americans think, even as far back as the beginning of the Republic.

Guare grounds most of his work in the twentieth and twenty-first centuries that he has directly experienced. But even as early as the mid-1970s, he developed a growing curiosity to understand what he believes went wrong with the American dream prior to his own life and to determine a point in time when it began to go wrong. In the 1970s he moved to Nantucket, the place of his family roots, and began to wonder about matters of heritage. Guare recalls a specific instance that triggered his interest in the effects of ancestry when he witnessed a Polish woman instructively lecturing her niece while walking on a beach: "That image of this woman and this girl made me think, where do we get our information about life? We all have to live our lives based on these little shards of knowledge. Half the time we have to make up our information as we go along, but I thought, how do we learn how to live?"[1] For Guare learning how to live frequently involves family, but the attendant questions then become to what degree is one bound by the beliefs and actions of forebears, consciously or otherwise, and to what degree can one escape, transcend, or overcome the often unsavory influences?

In pursuing these questions, Guare has also recalled a story about his own childhood, recounting how his father and old war buddies built a beachside compound they called the Dunes Club and weekly escaped the city to this idyllic world with their families. One Sunday Guare's father's best friend,

Danny, grabbed Guare and accused him "of filching his ginger ale out of the communal ice box which he needed to mix with his rye."[2] Tensions of various sorts had previously arisen among the band of buddies, and this accusation triggered a bloody, vicious fight between Danny and Guare's father. Nothing was the same after that day. Always looking for a bit of irony, Guare recalls that his dad began the fight with an old horseshoe in his hands: "The lucky part of the whole day was that my father dropped the horseshoe on his way to finding Danny. If Eddie [Guare's dad] hadn't dropped it, he would've taken the horseshoe and surely beaten the head of his best friend and ended up in Sing Sing, the same prison Eddie's boss, Richard Whitney, president of the New York Stock Exchange, had been sent to for embezzling the Exchange pension fund back in 1938. That was a possibility too horrible to consider. What would happen to us?" (10).

This passage is rich and revealing. The main point is that two friends, despite their lifelong bond, succumbed to a murderous rage, confirming a growing suspicion in the young John Guare that humans are not rational creatures after all. The more subtle point in the passage involves the luck represented by the abandoned horseshoe. The difference between a memorable anecdote and a case of homicide often has little to do with intent or reason. Each man meant to murder the other, but luck prevented that from happening. Does Guare himself have this seed of murderous rage within him? Where did his father get this impulse to kill? With the parenthetical note about a case of embezzlement that made national headlines, Guare escalates his story to a level beyond his family to wonder how criminals succumb to criminal behavior generally. Is it innate, does blood line play a role, or is criminality merely the result of good or bad luck? Then, reminding readers that he observed these events as a child, he includes a final, self-interested, and childishly egotistical question: "What would happen to us?" Larger issues often stem from small matters and always have personal repercussions in Guare's plays.

Guare uses this personal consideration of human behavior as well as events on the larger human stage to study matters of inevitability, luck, and change; the role of familial (genetic or otherwise) entrapment and free will; and unforeseen, uncontrolled twists of fate converting to either good or bad fortune. America for Guare is a utopia rich with possibility. But the history of both the country and the playwright suggests an undercurrent of irrational self-destruction. Guare sees the American Republic pursuing great things, but the realization of its various noble and selfless ideals are invariably dashed by human failing at a local level. What does one do after the fall, after a father tries to murder a best friend, after a country reveals itself to be on something other than a selfless path to utopia?

For Guare the result of such ponderings was a trilogy (later expanded and reworked into a tetralogy, then further reworked and restored to a trilogy), collectively titled *Lydie Breeze,* that has yet to be presented in full, partly because Guare seems unsettled on its final form. The plays follow a group of young idealists during the years of the late nineteenth century following the Civil War up to the beginning of the twentieth. The first play is set in New England in 1875, where an odyssey ends that began on a Civil War battlefield, worked its way through the New England utopian movement and its fall, and ultimately leads to quiet reconciliation and adjustment. In its way Guare's undertaking parallels William Faulkner's novels of Yoknapatawpha County, both being creations grounded in the realities of place and period but dependent upon the authors' imaginations to bring each setting to life. It also has the mythic feel of Eugene O'Neill's tragedies *Desire under the Elms* and *Mourning Becomes Electra* and Nathaniel Hawthorne's novels *The House of the Seven Gables* and *The Scarlet Letter.* The work also evokes the fateful and foreboding romance of Edgar Allan Poe's poetry, as well as the richness of Walt Whitman's prose verse. Guare even has his characters quote Poe and Whitman on occasion.

Lydie Breeze is the first of the plays Guare undertook to write, working from 1978 to 1983 to complete it. It is chronologically the last of the plays, an elegiac reflection on the hopes and shattered dreams of a group of young idealists seeking refuge in communal life and hoping to discover the secrets of utopian liberty. Louis Malle directed the premiere at New York's American Place Theater in February 1982. *Gardenia* (1982), which Guare wrote in part to explain the backgrounds of the *Lydie Breeze* characters to Malle, returns to the central event of the series that occurred twenty years earlier, where one friend murders another and destroys all hope of idealistic realizations. *Women and Water* (1984) spans 1861–64 and includes battlefront scenes expressionistically delivered while establishing the roots of Lydie Breeze's utopian dreams. A fourth work, *Bullfinch's Mythology* (1984–85), is set one year after the events in *Gardenia* and has since been incorporated into the opus as *Part One: Bullfinch's Mythology.* This incorporation includes passages drawn from the eponymous nineteenth-century anthology written by Boston native Thomas Bullfinch, which captured the popular imagination during the time period that the play covers. Insertions from Bullfinch's myth retellings replace an extended opening dialogue in the original *Gardenia* about the death of Lydie's beloved gardenia, a symbol of secret love. *Bullfinch's Mythology* is followed by *Part Two: The Sacredness of the Next Task,* which in a prior configuration was the play *Lydie Breeze.* The two parts together remain titled *Lydie Breeze,* while *Women and Water* stands alone but remains integral to the overall work.

Guare's continuing interest in the cycle's themes and extended efforts to recraft the material can make following its several iterations confusing. Robert Andreach has studied the cycle's evolution and concludes the following:

> Though written first, the play *Lydie Breeze* was to be the fourth chronologically in the tetralogy. The first chronologically was the third written, *Women and Water*. . . . *Gardenia* [was] the second play written and the second chronologically. . . . The play *Lydie Breeze* [was] the fourth chronologically. . . . Guare never wrote the third chronologically, *Bulfinch's Mythology,* as a separate play to fit between *Gardenia* and *Lydie Breeze*. What he did write or rewrite [appeared in 2000] as two plays under the collective title *Lydie Breeze*. Part 1, *Bullfinch's Mythology,* is *Gardenia* revised with significant differences; Part 2, *The Sacredness of the Next Task,* is *Lydie Breeze* with fewer significant differences.[3]

All this rearranging speaks to Guare's engaging and creative commitment to his material. The current result is a two-play rather than four-play cycle.

In addition to the cycle's evocation of many other literary works, *Lydie Breeze* can be read as John Guare's version of *Ghosts,* Henrik Ibsen's 1882 play about the inescapability of heredity. Guare uses Ibsen's famous specter of syphilis to highlight the effects of the sins of the fathers. He has described *Lydie Breeze* as "dealing with the shambling remnants of a dream and how children survive their parents."[4]

Bullfinch's Mythology opens on a secluded Nantucket beach with Lydie reading from that anthology of classical mythology about creation, beginning with "Chaos—a confused and shapeless mass."[5] The term is repeated again by another character toward the end of act 1, both calling forth the condition humanity strives to move away from in its effort to understand and then shape the world. Lydie goes on to read about the creation of humanity: "'The gods gave him an upright stance so that while all other animals turn their faces downward and look to the earth, he raises his to heaven and gazes on the stars.' And sees—(*She turns the page.*)—what? The It . . . what is the It?" (20). The empty pronoun baffles her, and she cries out, "God, give me your voice. Give me a sign. Let me hear *you*. The It. What is the It?" (20).

Lydie is the central figure throughout the work. At this point in her life, she is in her thirties, the daughter of a once successful whaling captain and a veteran nurse of the Civil War, and currently center of a small commune struggling to survive in a house on Nantucket Island. She is married to Joshua Hickman, another commune member in his thirties. The other members are Amos Mason, a slightly younger member, and Dan Grady, a member who returns from employment with the railroad, an ill-found fortune in hand. Joshua is completing a great work of idealist philosophy. He and Lydie talk ideas, quoting Whitman and Poe and dreaming of breaking the oppression of the local mill bosses by energizing the workforce with their plays and poems. The group met in the midst of the terrible Civil War carnage at Cold Harbor, Virginia; Joshua recalls the siren call of a Shakespeare-quoting nurse: "I have a house, she sang. Thirty miles off the coast of America. We'll write manifestoes and develop a society that will shine as a beacon to the world. A paradise of the mind. A garden of Eden" (31). Lydie completes his thought by adding that in their commune they will find "the magnet that will pull us together. The It. The Great Idea" (31). Their chief problem is financial: they need an income to complete their mission. Regardless Lydie remains a steadfast inspiration, full of faith that true goodness will prevail even in a world dominated by a "machine that spews out human beings like Carnegie and Jay Gould and this new man, Rockefeller" (49). Their homestead is named Aipotu, *Utopia* spelled backward. Another dream opportunity arises when Amos, who is part Native American, announces he has a chance to enter law school. He could provide great help to the commune as lawyer; the only obstacle is finding the money to fund the education.

All their hopes seem dashed when Joshua's manuscript, titled "Prolegomena to Duty," is rejected for publication, killing any hope for income from this project that for so long had occupied the energies of the whole group. Unexpected salvation comes in the way of Dan, a former member now returned with the wealth the group desperately needs. Working as a ticket taker on a passenger train, he overheard a heated discussion about political corruption and bribery that implicated Congress and the White House. One man suffers a heart attack during the altercation but manages to shoot his companion before he dies. Dan takes a bag of money from between the two men, hides it, and reports the incident minus information about the bag. Official accounts identify the men as "two representatives of rival railroads going to Washington to do some lobbying" (58).

Dan successfully absconds with a massive amount of bribe money and presents it to his friends. Joshua proclaims, "We can create a new world," to which Lydie expands: "Years from now people will come here. This house will be a great museum. When did America turn around and start taking care of its people? Nantucket. Eighteen seventy-five. . . . I want to study Italian, Joshua. I want to read *The Divine Comedy* in the original. We've been through *The Inferno*. Let's be ready for *Paradiso*" (62). Hope finally has a backer. Amos can go to law school, and Joshua can go to Europe to study the philosophers his rejection letter (from William Dean Howells) suggests he study. And Lydie can continue her work educating mill workers of their rights.

In the following scene, Beaty, the commune's domestic help, steps forward and recounts to the audience her immigrant origins, including the inspiring feelings she felt upon arrival. Even the letters *NINA* posted everywhere—short for "No Irish Need Apply"—did not dampen her immigrant spirits. The new world had mythological resonance: "I saw these people in the sunlight, acting out gods and goddesses. *Bullfinch's Mythology.* I took that book and I knew I was home" (77). Jeremiah, Dan's son from an earlier marriage (his mother has died), appears, and everything looks to be on the verge of becoming a brave new world.

Act 2 skips forward nine years to 1884. The set is a prison cell cluttered with a printing press, paper, cans of ink, and a guillotine paper cutter. Amos, well dressed and apparently successful over the preceding years, enters the cell looking for Joshua, who is imprisoned for the murder of Dan. Though imprisoned Joshua still holds fast to his ideals of universal human rights, converting whomever he can in the prison by teaching them to read. Even the prison guard is beneficiary of his good services. Amos is now a successful lawyer, planning a future as a politician. He is visiting Joshua to reveal that a copy of Joshua's new book, *Aipotu: A Nantucket Memory,* meant only for personal use, found its way to Howells, who called it possessed of a truly American voice and wants to publish it. The book is honest about Dan's murder, the source of the group's money, and its socialist aspirations. Amos pleads with Joshua to consider the memory of Dan, who cannot defend himself against the book's accusations. Amos then asks what the book will do to Joshua's daughters and to Lydie. Joshua, however, knows the real reason for Amos's pleas: "My book dents and tarnishes your rise to glory" (99). The ambitious Amos cannot allow the book to go public, given he is fully implicated in all the unsavory matters at hand.

Amos informs Joshua that he invested the last of Dan's money quite well, currently has an appointment with the governor, and intends to secure a pardon for Joshua—based on sound legal principles, of course—but only if he destroys the book. Joshua refuses. Amos fills him in on recent events, which includes Lydie's banishment from Nantucket, the result of her trying to smother her two daughters to death. The girls will be put into foster homes. Clearly mentally unstable, Lydie enters the cell, telling the guard, "Don't worry, I won't pollute your prison" (103). She tells all of the horror of living after Dan's murder: she "decided to protect the girls in the only way [she] knew how" (103) and to teach them that "the most horrid fact about living [is that] anything can happen" (107)—essentially that chaos rules.

Lydie finds out that on the day Joshua received his rejection letter, out of blind rage he turned to her favorite gardenia and destroyed it. She says that had she known, Dan would still be alive today, because she would have immediately kicked Joshua off the island. Gardenias figure strongly in Lydie's consciousness and throughout the play. The plant resonates beyond simply being a living thing, given that her father's ship, symbol of everything free, good, and honorable, was named the *Gardenia.* Joshua concedes that "the same petty furies that made me kill the gardenia, those same petty furies made me kill Dan" (110). Discussions of failed idealism—an idealism that for Joshua was little more than a blinding passion to follow Lydie—leads her to tell him to sell the new book to Howells, no matter the consequences, suggesting that truth is the highest ideal. She leaves, and Amos makes a final plea to reject the offer. Quietly but decidedly, Joshua cuts up the existing pages with his guillotine paper cutter.

The second part of *Lydie Breeze, The Sacredness of the Next Task,* opens with a haunting, nearly elegiac monologue by Lydie about her birth on her father's ship, the *Gardenia,* off the coast of Africa. The birth was attended by freed slaves from Liberia, who chanted her into the world with cries of freedom. The play's action then focuses on a fifteen-year-old girl with an eye patch who claims that her father tried to blind her "because I might see him for the evil that put him in prison" (153). She is Lydie Breeze's younger daughter, Lydie Hickman, engaging in a much-reenacted ritual with Beaty the servant, recounting her mother's suicide and father's impotent response. The women ask the departed Lydie for directions from beyond the grave. They specifically ask, recalling the opening of *Bullfinch's Mythology,* "What is the It" that Lydie Breeze wants them to recover (123)? Neither has any faith in men, perhaps as a result of indoctrination on the part of Beaty, who considers all men to be weak and failures in ambition. Scene 2 opens with twenty-two-year-old Gussie Hickman, Lydie Breeze's elder daughter, returned home from adventures abroad and now "living in Washington D.C., working for the government" (129). She is a modern woman, drinking, smoking, and using unseemly language that shocks but also intrigues Beaty and Lydie. She has arrived on Nantucket aboard the yacht of William Randolph Hearst, newspaper tycoon and power broker, whose support of Sen. Amos Mason for president gives him a great chance of success. Gussie is Amos's private secretary, and they have arrived home so that he can officially announce his candidacy. The dream of Aipotu has been pragmatically incorporated into Amos's political vision, but the compromises implicit in his alliance with the Hearst fortune are clear.

A dissipated Joshua, now in his mid-fifties and far from the strong figure he was in his youth, enters to hear that Amos is on the island. Disconnected from reality, he disregards his daughter's plea to support Amos, even though Amos won him his pardon. It is revealed that Amos's wife is institutionalized (perhaps with leprosy) and that Gussie is his mistress as well as secretary. Her moral direction has been replaced by a longing for adventure; she has met Queen Victoria and been to a London theater to see a stage production of Mary Shelley's *Frankenstein*.

As the conversation progresses, the cause of Joshua's imprisonment decades ago is revealed. Dan was Lydie Breeze's extramarital lover and Joshua's rival; their utopian embrace of free love had its limits. As Gussie tells it: "Pa killed Dan Grady, and Pa went to prison. And then Pa came home, and then Ma died. It was all for love. All for love" (139). A local youth, Jude, appears and makes small talk until a pretentiously self-conscious and emotionally charged letter announces the arrival of a man in his late twenties who "affects the pose of a dandy dressed in a black suit, a ragged Byronic mien" (149–50). Joshua is terrified, apparently having fearfully waited years for this arrival. Gussie identifies the man as Frankenstein in the London play she saw.

Scene 3 opens with the mysterious stranger and Gussie alone on the beach. The man introduces himself as Jeremiah; he turns out to be Dan's son. Beaty intervenes, somehow certain that rape is at hand. It is a fear prompted by the revelation that she was raped many years ago and infected with a venereal disease. She claims her abuser was Amos, meaning that he is likewise infected, a fact that may explain his wife's current mental illness. Now that Amos has returned, Beaty is determined to ruin him by going public with her long-held secret.

Jeremiah and Joshua exchange tense words, Joshua asking Jeremiah what roles they must now play and Jeremiah dramatically absorbing the moment in a manner that he has clearly long awaited. Much like Guare's father and his buddy in the childhood incident that partly inspired the cycle, Joshua and Dan fought over a charge of theft: Joshua charged little Jeremiah with stealing his bottle of Moxie. If Jeremiah had not begun to cry, the whole affair might never have spiraled to its tragic end. Joshua expands: "But you had to start crying. Who would have thought that Sunday morning caterwauling would end up weeping for an entire way of life. Broke up the commune. Sent Amos to Washington. Me to jail" (165). Jeremiah, however, tells him that on that fateful date, he was seduced by Lydie Breeze. He was shortly thereafter sent to Britain, but "before I went, it began to hurt down there where she had taken me" (169). Ultimately Dan is revealed to be the original carrier of the venereal disease, infecting Lydie Breeze, who in a fit of revenge she later greatly regretted gave the disease to Dan's son. The scene ends with a mixture of understanding, forgiveness, despair, and impotence.

Act 2 opens with Joshua in "a high mood" (172), dressed in his old ill-fitting Civil War uniform and apparently drunk. Gussie rushes in, accusing her father of ruining her life by having Beaty give her story of rape to Hearst. She says that Gussie is living "in the House of Usher" (176), an allusion to Poe's tale of dynastic death and decay. Jude reenters with a story of the rapacious Hearst party's bird shoot, during which they killed even songbirds in their passion to destroy. Jude tells what occurred when Beaty confronted Hearst and Amos on Hearst's yacht and then reports what Lydie concluded after she read Beaty's letter of accusation: "And Lydie says, . . . 'My father may not be a murderer. He may be the victim. And he may not be my father because in the old days it was a commune and they all slept with my mother and then they murdered themselves and killed themselves and picked up disease. And poisoned each other'" (177). The recriminations continue, until finally Amos abandons Gussie as Hearst abandons Amos. Gussie complains that she is, finally, her father's daughter, "a *was*" (179) whose life has for all practical purposes ended.

Scene 2 opens with Jeremiah's confession to Beaty that it was he, not Amos, who seduced and "poisoned" her, before he knew that he was infected by Lydie Breeze. Beaty's poisoning thus is indirectly perpetrated by a woman she has nearly worshiped for years. She appears to go mad after realizing she has hated the wrong man all these years and ruined his life with a false accusation. In the next scene, Jude reports that fishermen have found the drowned bodies of Beaty and Jeremiah, hands bound together. Lydie believes her mother came to take her but instead took Beaty. She grows hysterical, but Jude calms her.

The final scene opens with Joshua's congratulating Gussie for giving Amos's speech to the disappointed crowd in town. The speech expands on a metaphor that the United States is a yacht, to which proud Joshua declares, "You looked like the great figurehead on a ship" (190). Gussie seems settled into living at home once again, humbled by her time in the great world beyond. In an unexpected twist, however, a young inventor, Lucian Rock, arrives and is enamored of her. He asks her to marry, she accepts, and the two depart, as it should be, apparently.

Joshua is alone with his memories and takes out his copy of *Bullfinch's Mythology* while out from the dark Lydie Breeze appears, "young, radiant, in her nurse's uniform. She is followed by DAN GRADY and AMOS MOSES in their ragged uniforms. It's them as they were in 1865. They are exhausted and radiant with hope" (197). Lydie Breeze the visionary is again in her element, describing how the Bible was written in the wrong order: it should have opened with Apocalypse—something like the Civil War—and gone backward until ending in Eden. The past breaks up, and young Lydie Hickman enters. Joshua and Lydie share a moment, with her asking her father to "teach me" (204). He pulls out a copy of Walt Whitman's *Leaves of Grass* and tells how Lydie Breeze once read to him when they first took the ferry to Nantucket. He reads to his daughter as the curtain falls.

Women and Water returns the central characters of *Lydie Breeze* to their origins. It is a work packed with information, which at times makes the play difficult to follow, but the telling of the tale remains intriguing. Set during the Civil War, it begins on a battlefield and ends on the white beaches of Nantucket. Guare's production notes for the play indicate that unlike others of the tetralogy, *Women and Water* "demands an imaginative use of the most minimal stage elements. It's not a play about scenery nor the authenticity of props that will give it its truth; it's the actors' belief in those props."[6] The title refers to the promise made to troops that women and water were just beyond the picket lines of the enemy, a tantalizing lie that occupied the imaginations of many as they advanced into murderous enemy fire and were blown apart by entrenched opposition forces. The play opens at the 1864 Battle of Cold Harbor in Virginia, notorious in Civil War annals as the place Gen. Ulysses S. Grant sacrificed thousands of soldiers on repeated frontal assaults against an impregnable enemy. It was the Union's equivalent, in many ways, to Maj. Gen. George Pickett's Confederate charge at the Battle of Gettysburg, revealing individual heroism wasted in the ranks by foolish leadership behind the lines.

The opening scene depicts a company of Union men excited into action by Sergeant Bell and massacred by Confederate fire. Through the smoke a man dressed as a trapper appears, soon identified as Capt. Joshua Hickman by Pvt. Amos Moses. They are old friends. Hickman is a photographer for the antiwar Quaker Commission, and Amos, lone survivor from his assaulting Union regiment, is assigned stretcher duty. It later turns out that Joshua is working for the government, looking for evidence of leadership incompetence and reasons to cashier Grant. Death and continued homicidal charges surround them as they begin talking about the need for a truce to help save wounded men. Lydie Breeze is one of the nurses on station, taking keepsakes from soldiers who are certain they will die in the next assault. They ask her to send the keepsakes home if they do not survive; her petticoat is already full of orphaned items. Despite growing numbers of wounded and dead, supplies are slow to arrive at the front, though apparently the supplies are adequate several miles behind the lines at a nearby landing.

Joshua convinces Lydie and Amos to go with him to the landing to secure supplies, convincing a doubtful Lydie that she should use the collected keepsakes to bribe the quartermaster: "You're at a crossroads. Ask yourself which road leads to the greater good. Staying here in chaos or coming to the landing" (17). He further argues that returning the keepsakes to loved ones does little to save the suffering soldiers. Joshua intends to take his pictures of horror and criminal incompetence to the landing and then on to Washington to prompt an end to the slaughter.

As Lydie listens Joshua fills her with a combination of idealism and pragmatism, with perhaps a degree of cynicism: "Find the soldiers who guard the supplies. See what you can get free. Remind them property is theft. Tell them all men are brothers. In the name of social justice, they cannot hoard supplies. Cry out that ownership is slavery and you're here to emancipate the medicine" (23). She is impressed by his rhetoric but not so naive as to think she would get much from hardened soldiers with such a speech. Yet Joshua tells her to try: "You're a Yankee. You're from New England. You'll know how to bargain" (23). For both of them, the combination of idealism and hard-nosed pragmatism is a strength that makes them leaders and draws them together as the play progresses.

The supply-depot guard is Sgt. Dan Grady, sitting alongside a road drinking wine and eating roasted chicken, clearly a man destined to profit from any situation he encounters. Dan takes Lydie to the central depot, where his profiteering seems well known. It is a grim place: a nurse at the depot has decided to accommodate the wounded by suffocating them, drearily rationalizing that it is the best she can do for the suffering. Joshua suffers from malaria as a result of a previous campaign in Kentucky; Lydie secures him a dose of quinine. As camp life plays out, the two discover a mutual love for the poetry of Walt Whitman, while the less cultured Amos leans toward simple camp songs.

In flashback Lydie recalls a recruiting officer's visit to her native Nantucket the same day that her father's ship, the *Gardenia,* was sighted offshore completely consumed by fire. Lydie's brother, Cabell, managing to escape the conflagration to return to shore, relates an account of the mutiny that resulted in their father being shot in the back and mortally wounded. Abandoned by its crew, the ship caught fire and sank. There are questions regarding the captain's competence and whether the insurance company should pay a major claim for a lost shipload of whale oil. Another flashback to an earlier time occurs, where a younger, more vital Captain Breeze takes the stage and recounts the birth of his twin daughter and son onboard the *Gardenia* many years ago. The play then skips forward in time to depict the uprising on the *Gardenia,* including Breeze's suspicion of betrayal on Cabell's part. Before the long-suffering Breeze tells all, though, he commits suicide, apparently unable to bear the burden of the truth.

Act 2 opens with Lydie exulting that she has secured supplies for the wounded, though the feeling is diminished by her realization that Dan first paved the way by convincing his corrupt superior that she wanted a percentage of the profits and was prepared to scavenge from the dead and wounded. Dan rationalizes that the corrupt captain would refuse to do business with her if he thought she was unwilling to cheat and steal, given that safety in corruption derives only from implicating others as well. Ideals clash with cold, cynical business practice.

In the ongoing chaos, Lydie meets Moncure ("my heart"), a black youth who attended her father onboard the *Gardenia* and onshore the days following its sinking. She seeks information but is accosted by a mother and son foraging for food. In a bizarre twist, the two southerners live in an isolated and undiscovered cabin with cages that house, among other things, a pig, Amos, and Joshua. Ultimately the son shoots his mother, calling her a traitor, and everyone is freed from a circumstance that appears to be drawn in part from the Circe episode in Homer's *Odyssey*. Joshua apparently has the shredded remains of a truce signed by Lincoln, but he is presumed dead by his superiors, as is Amos. Lydie, further, has been relieved of duties. All three are free to do as they choose. No one knows what to do next, though, until Lydie proposes finding their way to Nantucket, especially since Moncure reveals that he buried Captain Breeze's ship's log (which contains the truth about the mutiny) in Breeze's coffin. Dan's superior, Captain McCloud, appears, and everyone humorously convinces the man that the pig roasting on a spit is Dan. McCloud runs in panic, and all cheer Lydie as the "Cannibal Princess" and agree to go to Nantucket.

Arriving in Nantucket, they discover that Lydie's house has become a way station for runaway slaves, with her brother's approval. When the group arrives at Breeze's grave, the captain returns to ghostly life and reveals that his son murdered the nonwhite members of the crew in order to gain a greater share of the profits from the ship's cargo. He demands that Lydie pursue the truth above all else. Cabell tells a different story: that the nonwhites abandoned ship (rather than risk capture by pursuing Confederate raiders), breaking the spirit of Captain Breeze, who then began writing a madman's story in his log. Lydie denies her father's madness, to which Cabell reminds her that she called Grant a madman—with apparent justification. In an act of dramatic theater, the risen Captain Breeze apparently stabs Cabell with his whaling harpoon. In fact it is Moncure who kills him. After discussing all the death, carnage, and injustice, they decide to protect Cabell's reputation by saying he has lit out to California and the prospect of gold.

They all burn Captain Breeze's journal in a bonfire, and Lydie announces: "We have achieved experience. We are transformed by experience. Not I. Not you or you or you. But us. On this beach. Right now. Together we're a great soul capable of doing extraordinary things" (103). She announces that the Bible was written backward, and the characters describe the progress of God's creation in reverse, "until there is only God. . . . And God uncreates himself. . . . And there is only serenity. . . . And the world is back where it was meant to be" (104). Lydie announces she now plans the "the commencement of a new life" (105), and all sign on to the idea as the morning sky along the beachfront ushers in a new day.

Rejecting the past, accepting the past, and repeating the past are variously presented in this epic saga, bringing into focus the matter of how or when a better world can grow out of an imperfect history. Can success be built upon failure? Regardless of the answer, it is apparent for Guare that the effort must be made, even if failure is perhaps an inevitability.

Of the 1982 premiere of *Lydie Breeze,* directed by Louis Malle, reviewer Frank Rich commented that like *Atlantic City, Lydie Breeze* "is set in another crumbling beach town of another era . . . but it is about the same dreams, the same ghosts, the same kind of metaphorical wreckage." He concludes: "*Lydie Breeze* is not, however, an achievement of the same high order of *Atlantic City.* Like Mr. Guare's other recent plays—notably *Landscape of the Body* and *Bosoms and Neglect*—his new one is a literate, ambitious experiment in which luminous and savage theatrical bits float within a murky, incorporeal whole."[7] Despite the play's many thematic allusions to Ibsen—most notably with respect to the legacy of venereal disease—Guare clearly did not follow Ibsen's well-made play formula, recognizing that the subject matter would not have been well served by such packaging.

In 2002 Guare accepted a commission from the Signature Theatre Company to write *A Few Stout Individuals,* which opened on 3 May at the company's Peter Norton Space. Though the play does not directly connect to Guare's *Lydie Breeze* opus, its thematic connections and nineteenth-century setting give *A Few Stout Individuals* the sense of being an extension of those other plays. The play is a creative reimagining of actual history, centering on Ulysses S. Grant in his final days of life. As such its focus is on Grant not as a Civil War general but as the less distinguished postwar president and failed businessman.

Ben Brantley assessed *A Few Stout Individuals* in a manner similar to Rich's review of *Lydie Breeze,* calling it "vivacious" and "overstuffed."[8] Brantley added that "it is so unmistakably the product of Mr. Guare's exotic yet very American imagination. This is as it should be." He acknowledged that the play "is sometimes delightful and as often tedious," but he seemed more willing to accept the playwright's iconoclastic theatricality and appreciate his unconventionality rather than resist its breaks with convention.

The play deals with Grant's bankruptcy but also imaginatively returns to better days through theatrical ingenuity that captures the memories of this once great, now nearly catatonic man. In 1885 the once-glorious home of Grant's large family has grown dilapidated because of repair deferrals due to financial troubles. Mark Twain is working with Grant and his family to try to salvage Grant's fortune and reputation through the publication of his memoirs. Everyone reveals different levels of parasitic self-interest, however; even Twain is bent on salvaging his own fortunes by publishing Grant's work. This dependency is strained by the fact that Grant is battling a terminal case of throat cancer that has rendered him virtually incapable of meaningful communication. His wife does most of his talking, revealing her own self-interested perspective as she both cares for her husband and controls him by administering to him doses of cocaine and painkillers. Each of their four children has his or her own agenda as well; one of his sons is determined to salvage his fortunes by securing dad's endorsement on another get-rich-quick scheme, for example, and his daughter has married a dashing young Englishman as a result of them both mistakenly thinking the other is wealthy. Grant's chief assistant, Adam Badeau, tries to control the composition of the memoir, including its style and tone, best described as second-rate British idiom that impresses those who claim to have taste but is clearly inauthentic as an American voice. Against this backdrop of a dynasty in disarray, Grant's memories make an entrance, specifically in the form of the Emperor and Empress of Japan, whom Grant met on a state visit to Japan many years ago, resulting in the best memories of his life.

Grant experiences the excruciating physical pain of his cancer, is barely at times able to communicate at all, and is constantly in a state of medically induced semiconsciousness. His imagination, however, remains as healthy as ever, and he can recall the past in every detail. His inability to communicate creates a chasm between his memories and the current world, however, making it virtually impossible to complete his memoir. But the chasm does not prevent Guare from presenting an on-stage world that creatively blends the highlights of Grant's past with his excruciating present. The stage blends two sets of characters from two different worlds into a fully integrated collage. The first act sets a tone of impending death and loss, followed by a dreamlike second act that is as real as it is fantastic, as if Guare is testing onstage how much reality and fantasy can overlap or even replace one another.

In an author's note, Guare reports that he glanced through Grant's *Personal Memoirs* when he was writing the *Lydie Breeze* plays looking for information on the Battle of Cold Harbor that opens those plays and influences the characters throughout: "Grant had been in charge. Grant became the symbol of drunken corruption and waste, the very nemesis of, the personification of evil for my characters who had suffered under him." He eventually read the entire work, though, and found that he could no longer conceive of Grant as a villain. In fact his reflections on the complexities of his life left Guare to conclude that "I was hearing . . . the twentieth century beating its fists against the nineteenth-century typeface of this book. . . . What got me was Grant's was not a nineteenth-century voice. You could hear Gertrude Stein in its locutions. You could hear Hemingway in its simplicity and directness."[9] *A Few Stout Individuals* accordingly became a commemoration of a misunderstood man whose humanity left him unprepared to deal with the ravages of a world grown cruel and deceptive. The modern world, in short, had overrun humanity's ability to remain moral, ethical, and comfortable in its own skin, all in the name of progress.

Guare notes that the play's title comes from a quote by Emerson, "What is history but the biography of a few stout individuals?" (6). He wrote the following blurb, almost playful in tone, when the director asked for one: "A great man is dying penniless, his son having squandered his fortune. A publisher offers the great man a fortune to write his memoirs. How will the family keep him alive to finish it? How will the great man get to his memory?" (6). This melodramatic description is in the spirit of modern tabloid media; the distinctions between Grant's private and public blur in large measure because increasingly omnipresent media images determine much of what is real.

The play opens with "an extraordinary masked apparition" (11), the Emperor of Japan, announcing himself to Grant, who responds, "I know who you are. Who am I?" Twain, listening intently to a wheelchair-bound Grant but not privy to seeing the specter of the Emperor, wonders, "Who am I? What is he saying?" (11). The nexus between the past and present throughout the play is the imperfect medium of Grant. As the scene unfolds, the Emperor makes an interesting observation: "poor Mark Twain. . . . He is not like you or me. He is only a writer. He is not an immortal" (15). This is ironic, because Guare contends that Grant became immortal through his writing, not his campaigns to defeat Robert E. Lee and the Confederacy. The "American" genius of Grant's *Memoirs* assure his immortality. Whereas in Japan the immortality of the Emperor is a given, for Grant the act of achieving the status of godhood requires the fickle, tempering flames of transformative media adulation.

The play alternates between the rich imaginings of Grant and the desperate attempts of his many hangers-on to keep him alive until he can finish the memoir. Twain, perhaps the last to learn that Grant's death is imminent, has invested his fortune in promoting a manuscript that he discovers does not exist except for the unsuitable version that Badeau has manufactured. Grant's son Buck has a "foolproof scheme" (42) to salvage the family fortune, but it was his earlier scheme that led to the family's ruin and damaged Grant's reputation by dragging trusting investors to their ruin. Grant's wife is hungry to return to her former glory as a wealthy socialite and herself schemes to profit from her husband once again. Desperation sinks in as everyone increasingly fears that he is incapable of completing his memoirs.

Act 2 opens with Grant again talking to the Emperor and Empress of Japan, Grant musing that "being with you [was] the last time I was ever happy" (55). The cultural differences this interaction highlights is key to the play. Unlike Japan the United States created itself from the ground up, and even the few stout individuals that are the backbone of history derive their reputations and historical footing from popular opinion, a fickle and unpredictable foundation upon which to build greatness. As Guare has dramatized in earlier works, even the great suffer at the hands of forces that extend beyond their powers. To some extent reputation is beyond control of even the greatest of men and women. Not only are ineffectual dreamers destined to disappointment; even those who have the world before them are subject to failure and bitterness.

Eventually stimulated by old stories told to him by his ancient assistant, Harrison, Grant rouses and dictates his story in an honest American voice that Guare calls "right up there with Melville and Hawthorne, and Twain himself" (8). The work bluntly and fairly faces all the other triumphs and errors of a life fully lived in sacrifice and duty to his country.

The play ends with everyone's future summarized, including the note that Twain's luck in business continued from bad to worse even with the money he earned from the success of Grant's book. The Emperor of Japan is remembered mostly as a character in the comic operetta *The Mikado*, hardly as the powerful presence he was in life. He does seem to be inspiration for something more, however, the figure that inspires Grant to turn to the present in order to recuperate the past: "Write your memories," he says. "Set them down. Don't let America forget the war. . . . That's all writing a book is: a letter to an unknown friend" (86).

A Few Stout Individuals and the *Lydie Breeze* plays look back at a United States reunited and regenerated after a devastating war. This brought promise of a new, truer union. However, Guare reminds us, those idyllic dreams almost instantly imploded for even the most idealistic of Americans, imperfect humans all. Good intentions cannot overcome the fact that even the best among us are mere mortals, flawed creatures, a fact that bodes poorly for anyone determined to find or create utopia. The urge itself never dies out, however, and that is both cause for hope and reason to despair.

CHAPTER 7

Six Degrees of Separation (1990)

Six Degrees of Separation (1990) boosted John Guare to a new level of fame in the early 1990s. The play premiered on 19 May 1990 at New York's Mitzi E. Newhouse Theater, Lincoln Center, directed by Jerry Zaks and starring Stockard Channing (who was nominated for the 1991 Tony Award for best actress in a play), John Cunningham, and James McDaniel. On November 8 the production moved to the larger Vivian Beaumont Theatre at Lincoln Center, marking its Broadway debut. It ran for 485 performances. It won an Obie Award and the New York Drama Critics' Circle Award, was nominated for the 1991 Tony Award for best play, and was a finalist for the Pulitzer Prize in drama. The play was soon performed worldwide and received broad international acclaim. The London production (with Channing and Ian McKellan) won an Olivier Award for best play. In 1993 a film adaptation, with a screenplay by Guare, was released, starring Channing, Will Smith, and Donald Sutherland.

The play's title derives from the mathematical postulate that everyone in the world is connected to everyone else by a chain of no more than six acquaintances. In act 2 would-be art patron Ouisa speaks to the audience, explaining the concept: "I read somewhere that everybody on this planet is separated by only six other people. Six degrees of separation. Between us and everybody else on this planet. The president of the United States. A gondolier in Venice. Fill in the names. I find that A) tremendously comforting that we're so close and B) like Chinese water torture that we're so close. . . . I am bound to everyone on this planet by a trail of six people. It's a profound thought."[1] To a large degree, this concept is the one that Guare has worked with his whole career, that we are all joined together, for better and for worse, and need to deal with the complexities of the world with a sense that other peoples' sufferings reverberate throughout, even to the point of affecting those who are seemingly insulated from the world by wealth and power. The American myth of the rugged individual clashes with this more complex concept of social interconnectedness, making accommodation of that individualist ideal in an ever more crowded world all the more difficult. Looking out for number one appears to be wired into the human consciousness, but it is an instinct that increasingly requires checking rather than encouragement. What Guare seems to suggest is that America culture, rather than providing checks and balances to our native instincts, actually condones and rewards those selfish instincts to the greater detriment of the whole.

Mike Vanden Heuvel elevates this discussion by applying information theory and related science-based chaotics theories to the play, plugging in contemporary theories of dynamic interplay as it relates to any number of science-based fields. Though change is an often dangerous process, Vanden Heuvel argues that it is nonetheless an essential tool in the evolution of virtually every dynamic system in the universe, from the universe at large to animal populations with their booms and busts down to activities at the quantum level. Human dynamics are certainly no exception.

Stasis is the enemy of change, without which there is no progress, though change can also have less desirable outcomes. The irritant (Vanden Heuvel calls it a *parasite*) that disrupts the complacency of the upper-middle-class world of the play and forces change into that static existence is a charming, homeless black man, who creates fractures that ultimately require new systems of understanding with regard to race, gender, and class. Guare is not, according to Vanden Heuvel, promulgating a "liberal bourgeois ethic of social unity" with a self-congratulatory play of union through better communication. That would be standard liberal fare. Rather Guare "seems more interested in investigating the dynamics of difference out of which increasingly complex (and complexly fraught) social relationships must emerge in partial and haphazard form."[2] Guare suggests that if progress occurs at all, it does not happen on a linear trajectory or follow a rational path to a clearly articulated goal. Progress is uncertain and sloppy and pays dividends in the least expected ways, including, quite frequently, not at all.

Vanden Heuvel's argument for *Six Degrees of Separation* undermines many published views that Guare is something of a liberal progressive who sometimes does not get the message quite right. Often the negative critical assessments of Guare's theater are based not on direct engagement with Guare's playwriting but on critical presumptions about exactly what he is trying to do. Most agree that he is not an absurdist celebrating (or mourning) people's anarchic inability to make sense out of life. Rather they often presume that he is a progressive rationalist who actually attacks the absurdism that was so popular in the 1960s by reasserting a faith in rationalism. This is a characterization Vanden Heuvel rejects. Playgoers looking for assertions of faith in rationalism will inevitably be disappointed because Guare's vision lies somewhere in between, as neither progressive rationalist nor nihilistic prophet of absurdism. Disorder for him is a state of human existence that provides an opportunity for creative transformation. Within that disorder pockets of order arise, offering momentary harmony before destabilizing into a new disorderly source of opportunity. Disorder promotes new orders; decay allows for regeneration.

Because critics and audiences are often looking for something in Guare's plays that is not there, they frequently miss what is there. With regard to the title of the play, for example, critics have focused on the six degrees, as Ouisa does, which provides a sense of unity hard to imagine in a world of billions of people. Though Vanden Heuvel never directly makes the point, his argument focuses on the word *separation,* pointing out that people remain separate however hard they try to connect. It is not, after all, six degrees of union. Rather than being a title full of optimism, Vanden Heuvel suggests that separation implies just the opposite of what Guare's progressive-minded audiences would like to hear. Separation and isolation remain the problems of the day, even though there is a tenuous sense of (six degrees of) connection. *Six Degrees of Separation,* perhaps more engagingly than any of Guare's earlier works, offers audiences the best opportunity to appreciate this agenda of separation even amid suggestions of interconnection. The play in turn does much to encourage a reevaluation of his earlier works.

Six Degrees of Separation has remained Guare's biggest financial, popular, and critical success. The play's success was also accompanied by offstage drama. Guare was inspired by the real-life story of David Hampton, an African American con man who managed to convince a number of people in the 1980s that he was the son of actor Sidney Poitier. Guare read about the case in an 18 October 1983 *New York Times* article. After the play became a success, Hampton sued the playwright, confronted him publicly, and harassed him to the point of making threats: "I would truly advise you to give me money or you can start counting your days."[3] A civil court eventually ruled that Hampton was not entitled to damages, but a criminal jury refused to find him guilty of any felony charges.

Like most of Guare's work, *Six Degrees of Separation* rejects realist conventions by utilizing direct address, lighting changes to indicate place and time shifts, and high-energy pacing. Gene Plunka summarizes Guare's approach in this case: "The Brechtian alienation effect of having the actors sit closely to the stage to appear and vanish at will, reinforcing the notion that the tale is being narrated as performance art, also serves to raze fourth-wall conventions."[4] The play is an intimate event requiring actors capable of making contact with the audience, of both telling the tale and acting it out. It is told in retrospect but given present urgency during the times it slips into "present" action. It is an engaging mixture of reflective self-assessment and spontaneous, spirited action.

The stage is dominated by a Wassily Kandinsky painting placed over the acting space, rotating to show both sides, which the artist painted, according to the stage directions, "in two different styles. One side is geometric and somber. The other side is wild and vivid." As the play begins, "the painting stops its revolve and opts for the geometric side" (3). This simple device informs the audience that of the two sides of human nature, they are watching the side that values order. The setting is a world of sophistication, and refinement will rule the day. Everything has its place, though as soon as Ouisa and Flan step on stage, things fall into frenetic disarray. In a frantic and extended opening scene, panic dominates the dialogue, spoken directly to the audience, informing us that a curious event the previous night left them exposed to theft and murder, though luckily they escaped unharmed.

In a mixture of direct address and reenactment, the couple recounts the exhilarating and then frightening events of the night before. Throughout one gets the idea that for this couple even the thought of murder has brought a sort of vitality to their lives that they had not experienced in some time. Art dealer Flan and Ouisa, his wife, were entertaining an old South African friend and millionaire (owner of gold mines), hoping that he would loan them money to complete an art deal that would save them from bankruptcy. Amid the small talk about apartheid and the responsibilities of those in power to guarantee the proper advancement of history, there is a knock at the door. A young black man named Paul claims to need help after being mugged in Central Park, just across the street; he chose to seek help from Flan and Ouisa, he says, because he is friends with their children at Harvard. As everyone tries to tend to Paul's wound, Paul claims that he is in New York to meet his father, Sidney Poitier, who is directing a film version of the Broadway musical *Cats*. Feeling better, Paul insists the group not go out to dinner but allow him to cook for them.

Ouisa, Flan, and magnate Geoffrey are charmed by Paul, a black youth possessing all the courtesies of upper-middle-class refinement without the anger, ennui, and resentment of typical youths his age. He speaks well of his elders and tells Ouisa and Flan just what they want to hear about their children at Harvard, describing them in terms that only desperate parents would be willing to believe. Geoffrey is won over, too, and in his good mood agrees to secure the loans his friends are requesting, even offering more support if needed.

The meal is wonderful, but the dinner conversation especially overpowers the adults. Paul speaks knowledgably and with warmth about his father, whom he will be meeting tomorrow when Poitier arrives in the morning. Paul is inspired by his father, a confirmation for Flan and Ouisa that parents and children can coexist—though this is not the case for them and their offspring.

As Flan and Ouisa recount the tale to the audience, hungry to tell all and undoubtedly pleased that they have such a riveting story to share, Flan continually reminds them that this high-energy flurry is not typical in their lives. Flan, formerly a lawyer, frequently checks their enthusiasm by warning Ouisa that they may be exposing themselves to charges of libel. This invigorating and terrifying experience seems to have jump-started a humdrum life, even though it is a life surrounded by some of the most inspiring artwork of the twentieth century. For this couple, however, the artwork inspires little more than an interest in sales potential and the social trappings that attend the life of an art connoisseur.

Brought to life by Paul's entry into their world, Flan and Ouisa are more than happy to accept his unlikely story. Poitier is coming to New York to work on casting *Cats,* a production Paul says will be important because in a world where everyone is obsessed with questions of birth and death, there needs to be a celebration of "the eighty years we have to live between those two inexorable bookends" (45). He promises everyone bit parts in the movie, and all are tickled by the offer. Carpe diem is the theme of his college honor's thesis (the only copy of which the muggers stole along with his money), on J. D. Salinger's *The Catcher in the Rye.* In an extended monologue that requires the actor to captivate the audience in the auditorium as he does his audience onstage, Paul observes that the shooters of John Lennon and Ronald Reagan both invoked *The Catcher in the Rye* in rationalizing their actions. He says he decided to study the text to find the source of the violence in such an apparently benign book: "It's exactly as I remembered. Everybody's a phoney. Page two: 'My brother's in Hollywood being a prostitute.' Page three: 'what a phony slob his father was.' Page nine: 'People never notice anything'" (32). Paul concludes that the book reveals that society is experiencing "the death of the imagination." After all, he asks, "what else is paralysis?" (33).

Paul continues his exegesis on current ills by explaining the effects of this lost imagination: "The imagination has been so debased that imagination—being imaginative—rather than being the lynchpin of our existence now stands as a synonym for something outside ourselves like science fiction or some new use for tangerine slices on raw pork chops—what an imaginative summer recipe" (33). Having reduced the term *imagination* to nothing more than "a synonym for style," he further argues: "The imagination has moved out of the realm of being our link, our most personal link, with our inner selves and the world outside that world—this world we share. What is schizophrenia but a horrifying state where what's in here doesn't match up with what's out there?" (34).

Without imagination, life is a dead routine of merely scratching out a living, hollow and meaningless regardless of acquisitions gathered along the way. Geoffrey is awakened by Paul's message and confesses that his seventy-thousand black South African employees have rights that he needs to honor. These are matters neither Ouisa nor Flan fully understand. Whatever fire these two have allowed to go out of their lives, however, seems to have been rekindled by their unorthodox, stimulating night with this son of Sidney Poitier.

Here is where everything goes wrong, the cause of the uproar at the rise of curtain. Flan and Ouisa give Paul a spare room for the night. Paul, flush with his evening's success, uses their home for an encounter with a hustler he picks up on the streets after everyone goes to bed: "I was so happy. I wanted to add sex to it" (108). Ouisa catches him in the morning, and Flan kicks him and his hookup out of the apartment. Still believing Paul is Poitier's son, they try to locate him by locating Poitier. It soon becomes evident that there is a bigger problem. Ouisa and Flan meet two other friends who have the same tale to report. Nothing was stolen, though, and no one was hurt. So what is the reason this con artist is working so hard to take these people in? Who is he really? Though no one is hurt, everyone is outraged and embarrassed, needing to nurse wounded egos and reexamine their liberal values.

Paul is eventually traced back to the high school the victims' children all attended. Ouisa's daughter discovers yet another intriguing tale: her friend Trent, now at MIT, tells her that several months ago he picked up a young black man for sex. In return for sex, the man demanded Trent give him information about all the rich people in Trent's address book. Trent falls in love even though he remains tormented that he is gay, and he thinks through a plan to make his life right. He will train and educate Paul and introduce him to his family: "I'll make you the most eagerly sought-after young man in the East. And then I'll come into one of these homes one day. . . . And I'll pretend to meet you for the first time. . . . If it all happens under their noses, they can't judge me" (79). Paul winds up being trained for three months by Trent but then disappears. When Ouisa hears the story, she calls Trent "the Henry Higgins of our time" (81), invoking the Pygmalion/Galatea tale that George Bernard Shaw updated in his play *Pygmalion*. As in most stories of this sort, it is the creation (Galatea) and not the creator (Pygmalion) that is most interesting. Now we know how Paul made the transformation. But what was his motivation?

With reference to his speech on the imagination (plagiarized from a Groton School commencement speech, it turns out), Paul seems to be energized by these high-class encounters, putting his imagination to the test and creating situations ripe with risk. The reward is stimulation, admiration, and a momentary sense of place and belonging. They are occasions for him when "what's in here does . . . match up with what's out there" (34), even if only temporarily.

For Ouisa and Flan, and the others as well, such invigoration likewise offers temporary synchrony between their inner selves and the world before them. They are the helpful souls they want to be, and they come upon the kind of perfect and grateful youth they dream of encountering—their own children are anything but thankful for the "sacrifices" they have made. Of course, the adults are anything but victimized parents sacrificing all for their children. Guare puts this before us in the form of a frantic phone conversation between Ouisa (and later Flan) and their daughter. Clearly hungry for attention, the daughter announces that she is getting married and running away to Afghanistan. Ouisa and Flan callously hang up on her, though, when a call comes from Paul asking for help. They are far more anxious to deal with the exotic than the domestic. Their daughter can wait.

Before this phone call, Ouisa and Flan share another Paul story that occurs sometime after the initial episode. Returning home from a trip to Rome (where Ouisa got to climb a scaffold and high-five Michelangelo's God on the ceiling of the Sistine Chapel), Flan is accosted by his apartment building's doorman, who condemns him for having abandoned a now-grown son many years ago. The doorman heard the report from a young woman, who reveals that Paul is claiming to be Flan's child from the 1960s when Flan was a freedom marcher in Mississippi.

It turns out that the young woman, Elizabeth, met Paul on the streets, and she and her boyfriend, Rick, took him in upon hearing his sad tale. They are aspiring actors fresh from Utah, and Paul intrigues them just as he has everyone else. The abandonment story bonds the three with a sense of the injustices of wealth. Then Paul goes into action once again. He tells the two that his father, Flan, has finally relented and will recognize him, provided he finds a way to get to the family seat in Maine. Paul eventually convinces Rick to lend him the money, despite Elizabeth's misgivings and warnings. Paul, however, spends it on a fantastic night on the town with Rick, seducing him in the process. Realizing he has been scammed out of all the couple's savings and suffering from the shame of the sexual encounter, the doubly shamed Rick commits suicide.

Paul reads about the suicide in the papers and tries to reach out to Ouisa and Flan for help. (This is the reason for the phone call.) Ouisa feels drawn again to the needy Paul, at once cautious and excited by the renewed contact. Flan is not so drawn in but eventually relents. Paul agrees to give himself up to the police (Elizabeth is charging him with theft) if Ouisa and Flan will help him. Plans go awry, however, when traffic impedes their rescue efforts, and

Paul's arrest by police leads to him disappearing into the prison system without Ouisa and Flan being able to discover his whereabouts. Not being family and not even knowing Paul's last name (or maybe even his first name), Ouisa's search for him in the prison system is futile. Rumors eventually surface that he died in prison, though Flan says, "I'm sure it's not him. He'll be back. We haven't heard the last of him. The imagination. He'll find a way" (119). This late speech reminds the audience that Paul once proclaimed, "The imagination. That's our out. Our imagination teaches us our limits and then how to grow beyond those limits. . . . If we don't listen to that voice, it dies. It shrivels. It vanishes" (63).

Flan's imagination likely long ago shriveled and vanished. Less apparent is Ouisa's condition. As Flan ushers her to the elevator, she sees Paul—likely a hallucination—in the pink shirt they gave him that first night; he says to her, "The Kandinsky. It's painted on two sides." "The Kandinsky begins its slow revolve" (120), according to the final stage direction, revealing the "wild and vivid" side that has been hidden overhead throughout the play.

In the movie version's last scene, Ouisa leaves a befuddled Flan and is shown walking down a New York avenue, future uncertain but imagination racing. In the movie the Kandinsky is also on display in their apartment, freestanding so that it can be lifted and revolved. Ouisa spins it frequently, repeating "chaos and order, chaos and order" as she exposes the appropriate side. For her, and for the play, this balance between the two, between the geometric and somber and the wild and vivid, is the human dilemma. Too much order has permeated Ouisa and Flan's lives for too long, despite their proximity to some of the greatest flights of imaginations in the Western world. Those artworks make manifest what is missing in the couple's life.

Another element of the movie is worthy of note. Ouisa and Flan tell their story to a varied and increasing number of fellow art lovers, all upper-class connoisseurs who hungrily flock to these storytellers at the gatherings they attend. Ouisa and Flan have come in contact with a vitality—a life force—that none of their clique knows directly but all are hungry to hear about. Paul may be gone, but there is plenty of evidence that he has breathed life into Ouisa, if not into his other "victims." Perhaps even to some degree, those who hear are captivated by this tale, perhaps taking a first step toward recognizing the value of change. How exactly does one change, though? The question remains unanswered.

CHAPTER 8

Four Baboons Adoring the Sun (1992)

Following *Six Degrees of Separation,* Guare's next full-length play was *Four Baboons Adoring the Sun*. It premiered at New York's Vivian Beaumont Theater at the Lincoln Center on 18 March 1992, starring Stockard Channing and James Naughton. Guare originally wrote the piece as a libretto for a Leonard Bernstein opera, and the final version still contains vestiges of that early project, complete with chorus, grand staging, and larger-than-life characters. Nevertheless the play proceeds from realistic premises. Though critics generally greeted this experimental piece with reservations, it received a Tony nomination for best play in 1992.

The script attracted the attention of British director Sir Peter Hall, who identified Guare's trademark theatricality:

> In some respects, *Four Baboons* is a masque. Its story—the hesitant meeting of two tribes of young children from previous marriages—is realistic and funny enough. But it uses that reality to climb into regions of emblematic theater that go far above naturalism. John's vision could only be fulfilled by using the full armory of theatrical techniques: direct audience address in which the actor narrates his past and yet lives it at the same time; choric speaking by the chorus of children, not only to maintain their tempo and inflections, but to emphasize their nature as a group rather than as individuals; and above all music, expressing, in more than twenty short songs, the mythical world through the mouth of the god Eros.[1]

Guare presents a thoroughly modern situation—a blended family—but strikes through the mask of realism by probing that reality down to its mythic core. This mythic undercurrent rises and overtakes a fundamentally domestic event, in this case a family vacation that is intended to cure all their ills. Hall adds:

"*Four Baboons* could be conceived of as high comedy about people who thought that the enormity of their love could let them make a Faustian bargain with the universe—their love gave them carte blanche. But Guare had set this comic world of high optimism and easy solutions into a dark world of chaotic life forces. These were represented by Eros, and he would be the only singer. Music would therefore play the roles of passion and chaos. And finally, it would produce reconciliation" (x). Thus domestic realism meets the elemental forces of primitive, prerational mythology. Music becomes the shorthand for that force, recalling Jack Argue's dreams of infecting the modern world with liberating Etruscan music in *Muzeeka*.

The play is set in an archaeological site in Italy. Penny and Philip McKenzie are recently divorced and newly married to each other. Each have had the lifelong dream of working an archeological dig, and they are awaiting the arrival of their children from previous marriages, who will all meet for the first time as a single unit. The play seems to extol the virtues of travel to exotic locales for purposes of self-discovery and personal revitalization. Guare, however, inserts extra layers of haunting dreamscapes and mythic primitivism. Against this backdrop the McKenzie family discovers how ill prepared it is to face the life forces they think they want to experience.

The play's text sets the scene: "Primitive and ancient sounds. The austere marble wreckage of Classical times."[2] Onto the stage "EROS rises out of the smoking primordial ooze" (3). In rhythmic incantation he observes, "The start of another day/Something will go wrong. . . . I do not control things/I simply urge them along" (3). In a move that is characteristic of Guare, Eros not only offers a choral incantation but also directly engages the audience:

> And who is it I'm waiting for
> (*He shines* [*his golden*] *disc around the audience catching their faces.*)
> Is anybody's guess.
> Is it you
> Or you
> Or. (3)

At that point Philip and Penny rush onstage, racing through an airport in anxious anticipation of meeting their children at the arrival gate.

Eros's ominous entrance establishes one of the two currents of action in the play, which Philip characterizes as Universe A and Universe B, representing respectively order and chaos in an expanded version of what Guare presents with the Kandinsky painting in *Six Degrees of Separation*. Philip describes Universe A as "all facts and reason and explanations. Every aspect of life dragged down with the same old same old." Universe B, on the other hand, is a childlike world unpolluted by adult imposition: “No past, everything free. Mythic” (21). Reflecting on his hard-to-manage children, he adds: “No wonder everything is different for these little monsters. They live in a universe that’s constantly brand new. No rules. All adults try to get back to that world. But you can only do it by falling in love” (21). There are clearly certain echoes of Friedrich Nietzsche’s Apollonian/Dionysian dichotomy, roughly described as the struggle between order and chaos, reason and emotion.

The love that Philip speaks of is not of the tame, civilized variety conventionally boxed and labeled by society as marriage. He likes to believe his new love belongs to Universe B (Dionysian), filled with passion and guided by primitive urges. Both Philip and Penny have previously tried that civilized brand. Philip was married to a stay-at-home wife and Penny to an absentee, philandering political-careerist husband. Once an item in their high school days, Philip and Penny reunite in their forties and recover a passion they had once abandoned, finding what they hoped would be a new, more vital life by giving up everything that has chained them. Furthermore Philip gives up his secure desk job as a college department chair, and the two follow their shared youthful passion for physically working an archaeological dig in the Sicilian countryside, vacationland of the gods. Both believe their new future will bring them the passion, or the Eros, that they have yet to find even in their new marriage. To complete the picture, they have flown their nine children to Sicily for a uniting of the two families far from America’s neuroses in a land of idyllic pleasure.

The problems of the modern world follow them to Sicily, however, in what appears to be the beginning of a story about the failings of one world and virtues of the other. What is particularly interesting is not that the play criticizes contemporary society but that it criticizes human nature in general, regardless of time or place. Therein lies the tragedy of the play, as well as the tragedy of Guare’s vision. The real problem is not that modern Americans are pursuing the wrong dreams, though that is a problem. It is not particularly a contemporary problem at all, in fact, but a far deeper, even primeval, condition of self-destruction built into the human condition. Universe A and Universe B are destined to clash, as are Nietzsche’s Apollonian and Dionysian worlds. And despite the dangers that attend pursuing a vital existence—captured in many of the Greek and Roman myths—order and control ultimately overwhelm such life forces, creating a sterile world of mere existence and a despair one step from suicide. Only an exceedingly small number of people find Dionysian pleasure, and then for only a brief moment. Human dreams of arcadian escape can never truly be much more than dreams, it appears.

Penny and Philip do hit upon moments of pure joy in the early stages of their time in Sicily, escaping the daily grind and recovering the spark of childhood while pursuing the life of their dreams in this mythic, timeless landscape. Philip's son Wayne and Penny's daughter Hal, or Halcy (short for Halcyon)—the eldest child of their respective broods—have succumbed to the temptations of alcohol and pot back in the States, and the parents fear for their futures. Curiously, when the plane arrives and the children complain about all the inconveniences of travel in a foreign land, Wayne and Hal defend their parents, even to the point of excusing their home-breaking infidelities. Penny and Philip are surprised.

Crucial to the play is the fact that it operates in two time zones, a narrative present and three or so years in the future. From that later period, Philip and Penny deliver commentary on the unfolding earlier incidents by way of direct address to the audience. There are no changes in lighting or scenery to indicate a time shift; the two periods almost seamlessly intermix. The effect is a continuous time warp that evokes the timelessness of Universe B. The inevitability of the present becomes more palpable because it is actually already the past. The play's structure generates a curious sensation of fateful destiny beyond human control, not unlike that found in Greek tragedies in general.

It is eventually revealed that, before the two divorces, the children had all eavesdropped on Philip and Penny's phone conversations and so knew about the affair. The two groups of children had actually become familiar with one another prior to their rendezvous in Sicily, especially Wayne and Hal, the thirteen-year-old leaders of each clan. Though there was initial outrage and confusion, especially among the younger children, Wayne—wise beyond his years—observes that the passion Philip and Penny are experiencing is what brings vitality to the living and "kept us healthy" (36) amid the corrupting influences of the modern world. He even chastises the younger kids, to Philip's amazement: "I want you behaving well and supporting these two magnificent people. They are working so hard to give us a life" (37). Philip, though amazed, believes he understands why Wayne is so supportive. He explains to Penny that until now "they've never seen love. All they knew about adults with me and Jeanne was hate and fury and rage and homicide. And what do they know about love from you and Mel? To hear anything about love can't be bad. We're the great model. We're the ideal" (39). Philip clearly does not understand that he is playing with fire.

Problems soon arise on the island that explain the significance of the play's title. Before their move to Sicily, Philip and Penny married in Paris and did some preliminary research in one of the city's museums, falling in love with a four-thousand-year-old granite statue of four baboons adoring the sun. Penny notes that the baboons' eyes are "running out of their heads with joy" (33), to which Philip adds, "Their eyes [are] burnt out because they've seen their God" (33). The point, of course, is that full exposure to ecstasy permits at most a momentary, blinding glimpse. What attracts also destroys. Safety lies in Universe A; the terrors of uncertainty lie in Universe B. Living in the Apollonian security of Universe A results in a life unfulfilled, however, and for most is hardly a life worth living. Philip's and Penny's earlier marriages are clear evidence. The risks of the passionate, ecstatic life require more fortitude than human nature adequately possesses. And even with what may be considered sufficient fortitude, the choices are rife with difficulties of their own, including the likelihood of a greatly abbreviated life.

The tragedy of human life is that both options are in their way unbearable. It is the message that most Greek and Roman myths relay, with their tales of mortals being ripped to shreds by gods and goddesses and ambitious youths flying too close to the sun. The myth of Icarus applies particularly to Wayne, who is randomly given that name when Penny has all the children pick new names out of a hat.

The path that attracts lovers and poets (and madmen) is that of unfettered passion. Having fallen under the influence of Philip and Penny, Wayne longs to pursue passion as well and finds it with Halcy. As they are only thirteen years old and are now stepsiblings, Penny in particular is mortified by the prospect of a sexual liaison between the two. Their connection seems to be something more than lustful adolescent infatuation, however, though Penny refuses to accept as much, planting her feet firmly in the mindset of Universe A and forbidding any contact between the two. Philip, however, is more measured in his opposition. His being more receptive to the possibility than Penny is somewhat ironic and in the end cannot be sustained. After all it is Penny who longed for freedom even to the point that she "wanted to marry an Etruscan" (29), recalling the impassioned joy captured on the Etruscan urns, so central to Guare's *Muzeeka*. She is also the one who, according to Philip, likes the risks of making eye contact in the Mafia-infested Sicilian countryside, where such an affront could lead to death. Penny is—or wants to be—a free spirit, unfettered and alive. On the other hand, Philip is the one who advocates *omertà*, the Sicilian practice of clan silence designed to prevent family secrets from going public. There is secrecy and even shame in Philip's heart, qualities that temper any aspirations to a free, unfettered existence. However one sorts out the couple's various differences, both Penny and Philip have a long way to go to reach the untamed existences they claim to want.

Their worst fears are realized in fairly short order. Regardless of parental efforts to control the children, Wayne and Hal rise to majestic heights and consummate their love under the watchful support of ever-present Eros. Earlier in the play, Wayne asked Philip, "Who was the Duke of Windsor?" (11), referring to the man who gave up the British throne to be with his forbidden love (a divorced woman). Wayne heard of the duke from his mom, who claimed Philip was like the Duke of Windsor. A comically inappropriate comparison with respect to Philip, it is actually more appropriate for Wayne, who sees his only authentic option as giving up the ways of the world and going all in for love. Philip shows his weakness, his basic inability to live in his longed-for Universe B, when he concedes: "I saw two inept kids going at it in some insane parody of Penny and me. Universe A? Universe B? Instead of our getting into the kids' world, we had dragged the kids into our world. For all our ideals, we had passed only our fever on to our children. I want life to have passion but I also want life to be sane. I started to run forward to stop them but Penny pulled me back" (6).

Philip only sees something sordid in a sex act that is played onstage as beautiful though dangerously illicit. He thinks the two kids are mere adolescent adventurers fumbling in imitative efforts to follow in the path of their own lust-bound but otherwise timid parents. Penny, on the other hand, has moved a good deal away from her middle-class housewife ethos to become more capable of looking directly into the stinging rays of a reality unfiltered by civilized formalities.

Wayne's final act is to try to preserve this moment of sexual and passionate ecstasy, walking to the precipice of a cliff, taking Hal's hand, and walking over the edge. But, Penny recounts, "Halcy pulled her hand away" (62), leaving Wayne to fall alone, an act she immediately regretted. Icarus-like, Wayne's ascent to ecstatic heights ends in a great fall. Like the four baboons adoring the sun, he will forever be frozen in a moment of fatal ecstasy. The family is crushed, and all romantic fantasies of joy apparently ruined.

Philip plans to return with the children and Wayne's body to the United States, while Penny stays behind with Halcy, newly initiated into the world of near ecstasy, a survivor drawn dangerously to the edge but neither blinded nor killed. Unlike either Penny or Philip, she has come closest of all to what omnipresent Eros summarizes: "Your eyes have seen into the heart, the heart of love / It was easier for baboons to adore the sun / Than for you to look into the heart, the heart of love" (69). Mother and daughter will try to discover—or rediscover—that heart of love, providing a continuum of hope for them and humanity.

Wayne was named after John Wayne, a paradigm of American strength and optimism, and Halcy's name is short for Halcyon, since at her birth Penny and her husband—a soon-to-be congressman—felt hope in the world's future. That world, Universe A, fails to sustain anything but an impotent longing for what is found in Universe B. Living in Universe B, however, exposes the daring few to inevitable incineration in the blinding light of the pure love that Eros represents. Either way—either a lifeless though prolonged existence or a short, intense flash of life—humanity is caught between two essentially untenable options. It is not so much a matter of making the right choice as it is that neither choice is sustainable if both longevity and joy are to be parts of the formula. Eros observes, "I do not control/I offer a choice/I say to your soul/Rejoice!" (69).

The choice is a tragic one, being neither right nor wrong but rather right and wrong simultaneously. This is the formula found in Guare's theater throughout. He refuses to suggest some naively optimistic path to happiness because in fact no such path exists, except for the odd, brief moment where glimpses of the impossible shine out and tantalizingly beckon one to an early though ecstatic end.

Sylvie Drake of the *Los Angeles Times* asked readers to "imagine mixing one's metaphors and doing it by putting three adults and nine—count 'em, nine—kids on stage. Imagine invoking the gods of wrath, music, Sicily and humor in one off-the-wall swoop. Imagine creating a comedy that turns to parable and tragedy"[3] This hardly sounds like the beginnings of a favorable review. But Drake goes on to see virtue: "That's what Guare has done in a bit of whimsy with the improbable title 'Four Baboons Adoring the Sun.' It manages to hang together, in its own screwy way, even as Guare and director Peter Hall drop massive clues, like boulders along our path, to make sure we follow their intent." Guare's unconventional theater demands precisely the playfulness of mind that Drake herself exhibits in her review.

CHAPTER 9

A Free Man of Color (2010)

Guare's *A Free Man of Color* (2010) opened with a production directed by George C. Wolfe in the Vivian Beaumont Theater at the Lincoln Center on 23 October 2010 and ran through 9 January 2011. It was a 2011 finalist for the Pulitzer Prize, which was won that year by Bruce Norris's *Clybourne Park*. The large cast of thirty-two, led by Jeffrey Wright, occupied an expansive stage and embraced epic material conveyed via farce, expressionism, comedy of manners, and straight realism. Given the play's focus on early nineteenth-century New Orleans, it was staged in Baton Rouge in 2012 as part of Louisiana's bicentennial celebration of statehood.

A Free Man of Color is a celebration of human potential in an imaginative world unfettered by the civilizing forces of order and control, continuing the central thematic interest of *Four Baboons Adoring the Sun*. Large and expansive enough to fill the Vivian Beaumont stage, *A Free Man of Color* exhibits the carnivalesque explosiveness of plays such as John Gay's *The Beggar's Opera* (1728) and the metatheatrical intricacies of plays such as Timberlake Wertenbaker's *Our Country's Good* (1988). Elements of farcical exaggeration pervade the play—an infantile Napoleon appears in a bathtub, for example. Anachronistic insertions pepper the play, from reminders that the horrors of slavery will soon divide the new nation and lead to a devastating civil war to twenty-first-century accounts of the federal mishandling of the Hurricane Katrina disaster. There is also a distinct indebtedness to the comedy of manners tradition of seventeenth- and eighteenth-century Britain and France, especially William Wycherley's *The Country Wife* (1675).

A stirring gumbo of comic effusiveness, *A Free Man of Color* celebrates self-invention and the full indulgence of the senses, embracing mutability, chance, and materiality and undermining the life-limiting constrictions of order, civilization, and law. The play's theatricality is more than simple inventiveness. It complements the play's many thematic elements, all of which involve the ideas of "play" and "show," including the control of stark reality through the game of illusion and the avoidance of the dangers that are part of the "real world."

Ben Brantley's review of the 2010 Lincoln Center production summarizes the play's debts and influences, including "all-time big-shots like Lord Byron, Euripides, John Milton, Molière, Napoleon Bonaparte, Barbara Bush(!) and Virgil. And Shakespeare, of course. And William Wycherley, who wrote 'The Country Wife,' the Restoration comedy that provides the plot—or one of the plots—for this tale of adultery, racism and the Louisiana Purchase."[1] According to Brantley, therein lies the play's problem: "This big untidy historical comedy is pretty much the sum of what it cites. And its varied quotations and nuggets of fact never cohere any more than that eclectic list. . . . Here, in his first new play on Broadway in 18 years, he seems less to be juggling than tossing bright balls of allusion and information onto the stage and praying that they'll land in a coherent pattern." Most observers would agree with Brantley that the play is eclectic and not at all tidy, but expecting coherency, one could argue, is distinctly at odds with Guare's celebration of disorderly freedom. The play almost *must* be untidy or risk having form defeat function. Guare admits that "there's a lot of chaos within [the play], and that does ask a lot of audiences," but, rather than tidy it up, he was fully prepared to accept the cancellation of a scheduled 2009 Public Theatre production. Patrick Healy, tracing the play's path to production, observed that "Mr. Guare, in his first remarks about his experience at the Public, described the proposed alterations as 'completely alien to the spirit of the play that would have had the effect of dumbing it down.'"[2] What was eventually produced and published is precisely what Guare wanted to create.

The play is set in a New Orleans creatively fabricated through Guare's sense of carnivalesque indulgence, with the distinct Latin flavor of its Spanish and Caribbean roots. In the early 1800s, Spanish, African, French, British, and finally American influences were all vying for the soul of "the free-est city in the world," a place of personal invention where "you can be whatever you declare yourself to be."[3] Guare makes this a world antithetical to the Yankee orderliness of, say, Boston during the same period. Rather than portray the New Orleans of the time as a vice-ridden, amoral non-Protestant backwater, Guare presents this land of swampy instability as a place of opportunity for men of adventure and spirit unimpeded by stultifying moral scrutiny. Force of will rather than moral rectitude rules the day. And race is a Technicolor spectacle whose tentative barriers can be overcome by boldness of character. The play's central character, Jacques Cornet, is such a man, a free man of color who declares that he stands before the audience with the intention of creating his own character and writing his own play of the world. He promises to do so on the present stage, right before the audience's eyes. In a highly theatricalized world of dazzling show and Mardi Gras extravagance, nothing rests on bedrock and anything is possible. This is the case in the theater through which Cornet invents himself as much as it as is the case in unfettered nineteenth-century New Orleans. In short Guare has written an ambitious play that confronts historical interpretations of an important but little remembered part of the American past and celebrates what theater teaches about life and living.

Guare's play blends the story of Cornet with a history lesson of the circum-Caribbean world around 1800. The audience is asked to "take off your twenty-first century glasses. See New Orleans as we who live here see it in 1801. . . . Imagine the unimaginable. Race is a celebration! See the lush palette of skin tones in New Orleans" (5). Centrally Guare introduces such well-known personages as Toussaint Louverture, the Haitian rebel who freed his enslaved nation from French control. Identity, liberty, self-determination are central themes, and Louverture's example stands out as paradigmatic. He dies a captive of the French even as the French Revolution's motto of "Liberté, égalité, fraternité" continues to ring out, a pronouncement that does not extend to the slaves under French yoke. In the United States, the paradox of slavery in the land of the free is wrestled with by the likes of Thomas Jefferson, the man who announced that all men are created equal but is haunted by the fact that he has profited from the sweat of his own slave workforce. Jefferson and his assistant Meriwether Lewis, of Lewis and Clark fame, also play an important part in the play. Napoleon is yet another putative champion of liberty who betrays the cause in his self-interested rush for supreme power. Guare hilariously lampoons the little dictator. To lesser degrees everyone in the play, fictional or otherwise, suffers from this paradoxical behavior, speaking out for freedom but falling short in its full implementation. The new hope for humanity, the American experiment, also stands out above the rest in its hypocritical posturing.

Guare's history lesson turns out to be as slippery and changeable as the city in which the play is set. From the perspective of Cornet and New Orleans, history looks completely different from what was reported along the Eastern seaboard of the United States. The carnivalesque encourages this unusual perspective: seeing the world from the bottom up, privileging the underprivileged, and giving voice to the unrepresented, if only for the moment. The lord of misrule dominates, and all rules are exposed to challenge.

To effect Guare's project, Cornet needs to be played with larger-than-life expansiveness as he assumes the mantle of lord of misrule and announces that the play the audience is watching is of his own making. He variously renames his play throughout, from *The Happy Life of a Man in Power* to, ultimately, *A Free Man of Color, or How One Man Became an American* (101). His wealth, wit, sexual magnetism, and full-bodied appetite attract, intrigue, and repel those around him. Unwilling to succumb to more modest codes of behavior, he masters the surface arts of virtuous appearance, cloaking stratagems of seduction in a manner reminiscent of the most memorable rakes of Restoration theater. He "appears, a dazzling piece of work," and announces in one of many moments of theatricalized hindsight, "This is the last time men will dress like this" (1). Dress and attitude are only part of Cornet's indebtedness to the Restoration rake. Informed of the stratagems of Harry Horner, the rake protagonist of *The Country Wife,* Cornet adopts the Englishman's disguise of impotence to fool the town's cuckolded husbands. Even (or especially) his own half brother, possessor of a mulatto "country wife," is the target of insatiable Cornet. This is only the most obvious connection Guare makes with the indulgently amoral British Restoration world. He acknowledges on the cover of his playscript the influence of playwrights such as William Congreve, George Etherege, Aphra Behn, Molière, and John Wilmot; their highly theatrical stagecraft is central to the energy and success of this play.

Plots of seduction intertwine with political intrigue; hilarious buffoonery, insanely a chorus of prostitutes, a comically caricatured Napoleon, the Spanish king and infanta, a wily manservant, a British prude, and many others are "liberated" by Jacques's charms, and impotent captains of industry are tricked like Keystone Cops at every turn. Nineteenth-century farceur Georges Feydeau even makes an appearance to call attention to certain tenets of the theater as presented in this play.

Amid the destabilizing effects of the play's buffoonery and comedy, Guare presents injustice and hypocrisy among the ruling classes for what they are. Perhaps most damning is the disjunction between the image of Jefferson as an American founding father and the reality presented on stage of his betrayal of the Haitian people struggling for liberty interconnected with his decisions to apply harsh American codes of slavery to the newly acquired Louisiana Territory. Guare suggests that the Haitian and Louisiana episodes were opportunities to slow the cancer of slavery and racism that scarred the United States for the next two hundred years. The play also reminds us that the Spanish government up to this period had indulged racial commingling, which broke the black/white dichotomy into a kaleidoscope of racial labels that virtually erased color barriers from cultural and business affairs—hence the label "free-est city in the world." But the United States is unwilling to follow the practice. As the fertile potential of multicultural, interracial New Orleans is ignored and subdued by the sobering influence of northern European and American Protestantism, so will the West be properly subdued by the same civilizing forces. The uncharted frontier of the play is a great, undefined whiteness to be explored, surveyed, mapped, and forced to conform to an order extrinsic to itself, an "American" order that includes genocidal actions against Native Americans.

And so too is Cornet ultimately forced to conform to an order extrinsic to himself. His determination to invent himself and his outrageously seductive triumphs cannot stand forever unchallenged, because the dominant culture cannot allow such freedoms without risk to its own control and profit. Ultimately he is captured, enslaved, and sold, ending a riotous play on a somber note and reminding the audience that freedom apparently must have limits when civilization is at hand. Such is Guare's take on the lessons of American history.

Cornet opens the play in spectacular array, assisted by his slave, Murmur, the two men displaying a comic tension as Murmur undermines but acquiesces to Cornet's promise of self-creation and celebration of "the sanctity of surfaces. The value of veneer" (2). Murmur's comic resistance—and his slave status—suggests that all is not well in this world. Cornet, however, sees such matters only as trifling disturbances to be ignored or overcome. He receives his freedom from his dying white father and wins an inheritance over his prudish half brother, who is white and legitimate. Others resent Cornet as well, especially those in power as a result of privilege rather than ability. For him life is all a game, with victory achieved through seduction and cuckoldry. His sexual prowess is confirmed by the exhaustion and delight he generates in the circle of resident prostitutes, Terpsichore, Calliope, Euterpe, and Melpomene, who resist the arrogant advances of Juan Ventura Morales, supreme *intendante* of New Orleans, because no one can satisfy like Cornet. Despite the resentment of the city's power elite, these captains of commerce remain bound to Cornet because of his wealth and grudgingly tolerate him since they are never able to gain the upper hand.

The extravagance of the opening scene segues into an ominous history lesson, provided by a free black doctor, about Louverture, the leader of the Haitian Revolution, whose victory over the French changed the course of history. Had the French maintained control of Haiti (then called Sante Domingue), they likely would have invaded the Louisiana Territory and taken control of the entire North American continent beyond the Mississippi River. The slaughterhouse that Sante Domingue became during the revolution (with atrocities occurring on both sides) aroused universal fear that enslaved blacks throughout the Americas might also rise up and attack their white oppressors. One such quashed uprising occurred in Louisiana, just outside of New Orleans. These events creep into Cornet's play against his wishes in the form of white refugees from Haiti fleeing to New Orleans, instilling fear and increased hatred of the likes of him.

The play packs in a good deal of information for the audience to absorb, but it is almost unfailingly presented in an entertaining manner that maintains the theatrical edge of the play proper. For example Guare allows Napoleon to present his own perspective on geopolitics in a manner that is far from tedious, especially with respect to his obsession with Great Britain: "I hate the British. I hate Shakespeare. I hate Chaucer. I hate Richard the Lion Hearted. I hate Henry V. When the future comes, I will hate Big Ben. Queen Victoria. James Bond. Charles Dickens. Florence Nightingale. British Air. Julie Andrews. Mick Jagger. No. I will like him" (12). Charles-Maurice de Talleyrand, Napoleon's prime minister, humors his master but convinces him to think beyond Britain as much as possible. The campaign in the West Indies is put in motion when, in a strange twist of history, Napoleon recovers Louisiana from Spain in return for giving the Spanish king Tuscany for his spoiled, misshapen daughter to rule over. But these negotiations remain state secrets.

At this point in the play, Feydeau enters and announces that "there is only one rule of playwriting. Character A says 'My life is perfect as long as Character B does not show up.' Knock. Knock. Enter Character B" (23). Immediately following this metatheatrical moment, Cornet announces, "My life is perfect" (23), followed by the knock and the entrance of (Murmur as) Death with the words "*Le Code Noir!*" (23).

Amid these geopolitical seismic shifts, Cornet continues his subterfuge and conquests, especially targeting his half brother's concubine (made "official" by the extralegal system of quasi-marriage between European men and women of color called *plaçage*), Margerie Jolicoeur. Cornet's inability to meet up with Margerie in private inspires him to follow the plot of *The Country Wife* and have Murmur circulate about town reports of Cornet's unfortunate castration and almost certain death. He also has Murmur secretly tell each of his rivals that they are his sole heir.

Everyone trips over themselves to serve their dying benefactor. They each desire his wealth not just for personal gain but for the purposes of fortifying the city against the coming unknown. There is, for example, the threat of disease arriving in New Orleans from Haiti. Shiploads of suffering individuals (all black) are cruelly denied entrance to the city because of it. More important are concerns about who will ultimately rule over New Orleans. Informants with multiple loyalties abound in this shifting political landscape, and Cornet is among those in the hunt for definitive information, using his confederacy of loyal wives to search out the truth.

Cornet soon discovers that Napoleon is on his way to effect France's "restoration of *le Code Noir*" (23). He tells the audience of the history of this code, reminding that its restrictive tenets run contrary to the Age of Enlightenment. Surely the French in particular cannot permit the reinstitution of such an inhuman system. Incidents in Haiti remind him, though, of the extent to which France will go to preserve control over the wealth of its colonies. Such a restoration will surely destroy Cornet.

Jefferson enters with his minister to France, Robert Livingston—portrayed in caricature—and gives Livingston charge to buy New Orleans from France. On the surface this seems like the kind of news Cornet would long for, since New Orleans would come under the charge of a young country dedicated to liberty and opportunity. As with France, however, the United States is not what it appears to be, at least not in matters of race and the profit that slavery generates. Meanwhile Cornet pursues Margerie as a dying eunuch even on the eve of a tectonic shift of the geopolitical landscape. France's loss of Haiti leads to its loss of interest in Louisiana itself, though the United States fears that the French remain interested in New Orleans, prompting negotiations for territories neither nation fully values since most of it is uncharted unknown.

But Cornet's sexual intrigues do not mean he is uninterested in geopolitics. Throughout the play he is obsessed with purchasing maps reputed to reveal the famous, elusive Northwest Passage to the Pacific Ocean. Cornet wants to discover the passage so that silks and other luxuries can reach him more swiftly. He parodies the desires that drove Europe's great age of exploration, the last frontier of which (in the 1800s) was the Louisiana Territory west of the Mississippi River. Cornet's eyes look westward, reflecting the same curiosity that Jefferson and his assistant Lewis feel on behalf of the fledgling United States.

Jefferson and the United States do acquire New Orleans and all of the Louisiana Territory to boot, prompting American uncertainty about what to do with this unexpected windfall. Livingston was to buy only New Orleans, but Napoleon was happy to abandon the entire territory for any sort of profit after he lost Haiti. Amid all this geopolitical activity, Cornet's life continues, though increasingly down a troubled path. His eunuch ruse is uncovered, and he is challenged to a duel by his brother, who discovers that Margerie has become the latest of his conquests. Cornet kills his brother, and the incensed citizens, who now realize the extent of his deceptions, turn on him.

Cornet abandons Margerie and Murmur as well, and Huck Finn–like lights out for the territories, into the great unknown of the Louisiana Purchase possessed only of his many unreliable maps and intent on once again reinventing himself. In the wilderness he meets Meriwether Lewis, who tells him there is no need to fear the French Code Noir any longer because the United States now controls New Orleans. When Cornet asks Lewis about slavery, Lewis hands him Jefferson's Declaration of Independence. It is assumed that the creator of such a document that delineates the rights of man will take this great opportunity to realize those ideals. "Slavery will end," says Lewis. "After four hundred years of hoping, we'll find the western waterway. The world is falling into place. Go back home. Be part of the new world's bravery" (86–87). Slavery does not end immediately, though. The waterway is never discovered, and a despairing Lewis commits suicide soon after his encounter with Cornet.

Cornet returns energized, expecting New Orleans to have returned to its former glory. Instead he sees his band of prostitutes garbed in penitent clothing of the nunnery, his married mistresses abandoned by their husbands, and his black friend Dr. Toubib reclaimed by his Boston master. None of this seems to buckle Cornet, however, who shouts out, "We are in an Illyrian time. The golden age begins! Raise the American flag! Hurry! Let the freedom begin!" (89). Instead of celebration, however, the ghost of Cornet's brother enters "to witness [his] destruction" (89). An American Flag does fill the stage just as Cornet's many enemies seize and shackle him. His presence, it turns out, was revealed by Murmur, who is rewarded with his freedom. "I am now a free man of color," he proclaims, "I find that *very* nice" (90).

Cornet is sold at auction along with the rest of his property, of which he is now just one more item. Invoking the fact that "this is my play" (92), he demands to speak to Jefferson, and Jefferson, a bit disoriented, appears. While Cornet's abusers echo Shylock's speech from *The Merchant of Venice*—"if you prick us do we not bleed. . . . If you wrong us shall we not revenge?" (92), Jefferson vaguely observes to him that someday "you'll have your turn" (92). The world is not ready for emancipation.

Curiously, amid all the pleas, Cornet tells of a side of himself that has otherwise yet to show: that of business genius. He asserts that instead of having been "given" his freedom because of a father's love for his illegitimate son, his mother was sold away, and he was left abandoned and alone. Necessity forced him to earn his freedom: "In New Orleans, you'll see iron wrought into vines, decorating each building. I instituted that factory. I have a talent for alchemy. That's how I purchased my freedom" (93). His difficult beginnings give him an added dimension: behind the surface of this ingenious sensualist is a foundation of creative industry.

Jefferson distances himself from his Declaration of Independence, noting that "the Constitution is where we keep the laws" (93) and following with a discourse on the economic necessity of slavery and words of reassurance: "Patience. It'll happen. Have faith" (95). The words are small consolation for those who must wait, however. Guare has Cornet step outside of his time to beg Jefferson: "Change the future, now. You'll avoid a Civil War—Jim Crow—Dred Scott—lynching—back of the bus—whites only—assassination—degradation" (96).

Because of slavery Cornet has lost control of his play. He is given new pages to add as Lewis enters and learns from the script that this is supposed to be his last night on earth. Lewis and Cornet commiserate, two idealists crushed by the real world. After being sold into slavery, Cornet ultimately escaped into the great western expanse. Dr. Toubib returns to tell the audience that "perhaps his son returned years later as Nat Turner, or as Malcolm—as any many who tried to make those words 'All men are created equal' literal" (100). Cornet gets to look into the future in a last, ghostly speech: "I see visions of the future when generations of Margeries and Murmurs and Dr. Toubibs and the girls of Mme. Mandragola will be trapped on rooftops in New Orleans, reaching up to heaven to be saved. I say those bitter words 'Hang on!' And while I hang, I think about a time I had my maps, when I wrote my plays, when New Orleans meant paradise . . ." (100). A short scene follows that returns the characters to the happy times that open the play.

A Free Man of Color is an ambitious venture, funny and poignant, carnivalesque and amorally indulgent while also being intellectually, politically, and philosophically challenging. Joanna Mansbridge, in a scholarly article on the play titled "Racing toward History: Utopia and Progress in John Guare's *A Free Man of Color*," aptly summarizes that "*Free Man* stages a metatheatrical duel between two competing forces of history: one grounded in Enlightenment (rational linear movement toward an end goal), the other in utopia (an imagined future always in process)."[4] She concludes by noting that "Cornet's vision and our vision of him open a theatrical space in which the audience sees that recognizing history in the present is the condition of possibility for future change" (434).

The size and ambition of the play speaks to Guare's continued mastery of the theater and also to the frequently noted collaborative fit between Guare and director George C. Wolfe, whose input extended far beyond mounting the play. Much more ambitious than most current theater, *A Free Man of Color* is a highly theatrical masterwork.

In 2012 Guare's next work, *Are You There Yet, Mr. McFee?*, premiered at the McCarter Theatre in Princeton, New Jersey. This frenetic fable rivals and perhaps even surpasses *A Free Man of Color* in terms of freewheeling, nonlinear structure and narrative and *The House of Blue Leaves* when it comes to realism spiced with absurdism. Critic Charles Isherwood observes that "whiplash is inevitable after viewing this intermittently exhilarating, more often exasperating, comic fantasy about the terrors of childhood, the confusions of adulthood, the long reach of art into the lives of common folk, murder, screenwriting, the game-changing movie 'Jaws' and . . . wait, I'm getting dizzy."[5] Amid his reported disorientation, he added, "Did I mention that a giant Walt Disney puppet makes an appearance, trying to kidnap a couple of tykes whose bedtime reading material is not Dr. Seuss but Primo Levi's horror stories from Auschwitz? Or that puppet versions of Jorge Luis Borges, Jane Fonda and Robert Redford also figure in the plot?"

The play is controlled by Mundie, a playwright, who tells tales to a cocktail party of eager listeners. Mundie circles to a single incident that took place in 1975 when he used money from his first successful play to buy a Nantucket home. He discovers, however, that the current residents apparently distribute child pornography from the house and so he must fly there to sort matters out. Upon landing Mundie bumps into McPhee, whose own history mirrors his, including having a mistress named Antonia. McFee's Antonia turns out to live in town under another name with her husband and family; she may or may not have been pushed out of a window by her husband. She is also the daughter of the celebrated children's writer who once lived in Mundie's new house. McFee, and everyone else Mundie meets, previously performed in a local production of Mundie's hit play. He hears from his lawyer—whose wife is Antonia, his mistress—that he has been offered the job of doing a rewrite of Alfred Hitchcock's *Suspicion.*

Continual references to children's literature—including an effort to sell the children's writer's stories to Disney—help the play illustrate its own version of the inevitable fall of children from innocence to experience and present the debate of protecting or preparing them for that fall. Surrealism, including the work of René Magritte, becomes a major topic, as does the Holocaust ("Walt Disney is God's apology for the Holocaust," says one of the characters), creating a frank though dark vision of what is necessary to face the world as one grows up.

In his review Isherwood noted that Guare, Mundie, and McFee share many similar qualities: "'I swim in an ocean of stories,' Mundie says in the play's opening scene, explaining his vocation. Mr. Guare certainly has been profitably doing the same for several decades." Isherwood, however, was less laudatory in his judgment of *Are You There, Mr. McFee?,* citing multiple references in the play to *Jaws* to craft his conclusion: "But while he [Guare] is happy to be doing the backstroke in circles out there in the deep blue, he does not seem to notice the great white shark of incoherence trailing him from below. Or that his audience is sometimes unhappily at sea, not waving but drowning."

CHAPTER 10

A Career of Short Works

Throughout his career Guare has been interested in the short play. The form provides opportunity for playful (though often serious) experimentation in a concentrated format and does not necessarily require the embellishments of sustained narrative or extended action. The experiment can be undertaken, the effect created, and the task completed. There is the additional advantage of production viability: the cost of mounting shorter works is far less exorbitant and risky for backers than that of full-length productions.

Though Guare's fascination with the short play existed at the start his career, his interest has remained keen, partly because of his work as playwriting instructor at Yale University, where exercises in the short form occupied a great deal of his class time with students. The result is a feedback loop wherein Guare taught his students and his students' work inspired his own. His tendency to experiment—a hallmark of his career—makes him particularly well suited to teaching, and numerous student testimonials highlight his encouragement of their achievements. Rather than instilling a sense, for example, of the well-made play and the hallowed traditions of the theater, Guare encourages breaking with tradition and convention, to the delight of his apprentices. In the process his own body of short works reflects this urge for the new. It should be added that his status as one of the giants of the American stage—with a reputation for personal accessibility—has resulted in numerous invitations (which Guare often accepts) to contribute to short-play festivals, special benefits, and commissioned collections. Reviewing Guare's *Are You There Yet, Mr. McFee?,* Charles Isherwood makes a point relevant to Guare's entire career, up to and including his later plays: "At an age when some writers would be decorously guarding their reputations, he is still writing as he did in his youth, with so many mad fancies filling his mind that he can't always succeed in assembling them into cogent dramatic form."[1] Going small allows Guare to give birth to his many mad fantasies.

Guare's 1985 *The Talking Dog* was commissioned as part of a project titled *Orchards,* a collection of new short plays inspired by the stories of Anton Chekhov. That Chekhov has been Guare's idol since the beginning of his career surely made the invitation a particularly exciting opportunity. The plan was to have each commissioned playwright select one of Chekhov's celebrated stories and use it as inspiration to write their own work. The contributors were Guare, Maria Irene Fornés, Spalding Gray, David Mamet, Wendy Wasserstein, Michael Well, and Samm-Art Williams. The project, directed by Robert Falls, was organized by the Acting Company. The production went on tour throughout the United States during the 1985–86 season, and the collection was published.

The Talking Dog, based on Chekhov's short story "A Joke," is a dialogue between M and F and includes two nonspeaking parts for actors dressed as hang gliders. M is teaching F to hang glide. F takes her first plunge into the sport, is frightened, but loves the rush. As F flies (wrapped in the embrace of one of the hang gliders), M calls out, "I love you," but disclaims saying anything when F asks him about it. F launches again, and she hears the words again. M relates a curious story about a friend of his who trained her dog to growl out "Hello I love you."[2] Then he tells F that he is moving from his current location and will no longer be able to see her. The play concludes with a monologue by M about failed relationships, with clear signs he was attracted to F, but "I'd just as soon live alone as live with somebody who couldn't take a . . . joke" (139). The play works at more than the dialogic level. It includes the dancelike choreography of M and F as well as the give-and-take of the human gliders. The intermingling of love and nature, nature as love and vice versa, and the gliders' embrace of M and F all generate a sensuality that is fleeting and therefore always a bit tragic. Guare's hint of something extra that transcends mundane reality captures the spirit of Chekhov nicely. The protagonist's inability to capitalize on a rare opportunity—opting for escape and comforting rationalizations instead—is likewise quite Chekhovian.

Guare is particularly inclined to find time to contribute short pieces to special benefits, almost all involving support for the arts. In 1992 *New York Actor* premiered as a one-act play (later expanded) as part of a benefit for the American Repertory Theater in Cambridge, Massachusetts. The play opens in a New York theater bar that includes a "disaster wall" with posters of great theater failures and a group of young actors, including one recently returned from Los Angeles. Discussions include differences between the acting worlds of the two coasts. A crisis arises as a critic's wife's purse goes missing at a nearby table, with finger pointing and meltdowns abounding. A confession and apologies reveal the fragile grips these characters have on their careers and their lives.

In 1998 *Greenwich Mean* was also commissioned and produced by the American Repertory Theater for a short-play festival. Couple A and B romantically coo over each other as they move into their new apartment, spouting such phrases as "Love is the ultimate expression of time"; "I meet you. The Big Bang"; and "As long as we love, time stays in front of us."[3] An earthquake interrupts the love talk for thirty-five seconds, during which time the male, A, panics, screams, and grabs his possessions rather than trying to protect B. Though B reports, "I did not leave immediately" (28), the illusion of courtly honor and romantic love is shattered.

Another festival contribution, the one-act *Woman at a Threshold, Beckoning,* was performed at Marathon 2003, the twenty-sixth annual Festival of One-Act Plays, Series B (June), E.S.T. Theatre, New York. Other contributors to the festival included Tina Howe, Leslie Ayvazian, Lynn Rosen, and Amy Staats. Focusing on the war on terror, the play centers on the interrogation of an Egyptian woman suspected of terrorist connections. It moves from a courtroom to ground zero at the site of the former World Trade Center to the streets of Cairo, asking what one reviewer called "unanswerable questions about finding God and giving meaning to life."[4] John, a juror, agonizes over the trial of the woman, sympathetic to a point because he was practiced in the ways of mystical whirling dervishes. In a moment of befuddled enlightenment, he observes, "I know it's not possible but is it possible just to rethink it? That all of those thousands of people that day did not die in terror, but rather were—*struck* by a moment of ecstasy."[5] True to his habit of taking sometimes even dangerous perspectives on life, here Guare works to rehumanize a group of humans who were thoroughly demonized by the events of 9/11.

In 2007 Guare's *Blue Monologue* was produced as part of a collection titled *Five Story Walk-up,* which was compiled and produced by Daniel Gallant on 21 March at the Thirteenth Street Repertory Theatre in New York. It was designed as a benefit to save the theater from demolition. Centering on the theme of home and what it means, Guare was joined by contributors Neil LaBute, Quincy Long, Laura Shaine, Daniel Frederick Levin, Clay McLeod Chapman, and Gallant. Guare's piece is an autobiographical monologue about what it was like to grow up in Queens, which was initially something of a bedroom community; about his 1965 trip to Rome even as the Pope was traveling to the United States; and how in 1966 he began writing *The House of Blue Leaves,* properly launching a life where home for Guare became the theater.

In 2010 Guare joined company with the same group of playwrights, coordinated again by Gallant. He contributed the monologue *What It Was Like* for a production titled *Seven Card Draw* at Dixon Place in Manhattan's Lower East Side on 16–18 March. *Seven Card Draw,* the theme of which was risk and its rewards, was mounted to raise funds to help complete the multiarts performance space Dixon Place. Guare's monologue, again autobiographical, recounts events that figure in several of his earlier plays pertaining to what it was like to live in New York City during the crime-infested 1970s and relates the curious fact that he once lived in an apartment previously occupied by John Lennon. He concludes: "That's what I like about New York City—it's always being reborn, it's always reinventing itself. And it demands the same of you—that you keep readjusting to time. You can't live in the past in this city; it's just not there anymore."[6]

In 2011 *Elzbieta Erased* was commissioned by the Atlantic Theater Company in New York. It premiered on 18 May and then moved briefly to an art gallery on Vinalhaven Island, Maine, to be performed in front of the haunting portrait that is central to the play, before officially opening at the Atlantic Theater Company. This production marked Guare's acting debut, as "A," one of the play's two roles. In 2013 *Elzbieta Erased* was restaged at the Atlantic Theater Company under the umbrella title *3 Kinds of Exile* along with two additional Guare pieces, *Karel* and *Funiage.* Guare reprised his performance as A for the latter production. Each piece in *3 Kinds of Exile* centers on the experiences of an Eastern European exile to the United States.

Karel is a monologue reminiscence of an old friend of Guare's—director Karel Reisz (who directed Guare's *Gardenia*)—who in the 1930s was a Kindertransport exile and in the 1950s developed a strange and incurable rash. The flashback, tale-within-a-tale summary of Reisz's traumatic, war-infested memories brilliantly exhibits what Alexis Soloski calls "Guare's cunning intelligence and rich descriptive powers, as in the depiction of a psychosomatic rash: 'He felt like an Easter egg someone had dipped into fuchsia. He felt like a tropical flower out of Gauguin. He felt his body was the red of anger.'"[7]

Elzbieta Erased is a lecture-like dialogue detailing the life of the late Elzbieta Czyzewska, a Polish film and theater star whose talents were lost in translation when she married journalist David Halberstam in 1965 and moved with him to New York City. Struggles with Communist control followed by struggles with American lack of control, moving from national celebrity status to near oblivion, mark Czyzewska's story as one Guare felt compelled to write and present.

Funiage, perhaps the least successful of the three pieces, is a stylistic mashup somewhat reminiscent of *A Free Man of Color* in that it is a comically absurd bio-musical, frenetically produced to induce broad laughter. The play is about Witold Gombrowicz, an experimental Polish novelist and playwright (one of Guare's heroes) who left his home country in 1939, never to return. Grasping the idea that exile is a sort of death and rebirth—the play's title is a fusion of *funeral* and *marriage*—Gombrowicz learns that it demands reinvention, an insight he struggles to embrace fully.

In 2012 *The Sea,* a ten-minute monologue, was produced at a benefit for the Red Bull Theater at New York's St. Clement's Church. The speaker is dressed as a sea captain, speaking as if he were a seaman currently living in a submarine, yet he is clearly a prison inmate serving time for illegal financial transactions. He reports that his reputation followed him to prison, where he presumably resumes his Ponzi schemes bilking prisoners and guards alike. The work is evocative in tone, ghostly even, and anything but realistic in nature. What may be of particular interest, however, is that Guare has shared his talents once again for a benefit supporting a theater group. The Red Bull Theater describes itself as "dedicated to the presentation of vital and imaginative productions of heightened language plays. . . . Red Bull Theater engages the intellect and imagination of today's theatergoers through intimate and evocative stagings of great classic stories from all eras and cultures."[8]

In 2014 Daniel Gallant again procured Guare's talents and produced *Between* as part of an evening of short plays called *Nine Signs of the Times.* It played 11–13 April at the Nuyorican Poets Café in New York as a fund-raiser for the café's daytime and afterschool literacy and performance programs. Other contributors included Neil LaBute, Caridad Svich, Halley Feiffer, Quincy Long, Laura Shaine, Clay McLeod Chapman, Daniel F. Levin, and Gallant. In June 2014 the Theater Breaking Through Barriers produced *Between* at Theatre Row's Clurman Theatre in New York as part of an evening called *Power Plays,* TBTB's fourth annual short-play festival. Again Guare shows his interest in and concern for social causes, as TBTB is dedicated to advancing artists with disabilities and changing the image of people with disabilities from dependence to independence. Other contributors included LaBute, Bekah Brunstetter, Bruce Graham, and David Henry Hwang. The TBTB production also toured Japan in October 2014. On 3 November 2014 *Between* reunited Guare with Stockard Channing, who performed the play at NeueHouse in New York City. In an echo of the world found in *Six Degrees of Separation, Between* was mounted (with Jack O'Brien directing) to commemorate the thirtieth anniversary of NeueHouse's opening and the publication of the book *What If . . . ? The Architecture and Design of David Rockwell.*

The play is set in a restaurant with two people at a table confessing past transgressions as they absorb the transformative vibes of their surroundings.

Discussion turns to a long-ago visit to Egypt. B tells A about the tour guide's lecture: "This tomb, this king. See his bird head. That is his Ba. We all have a Ba. Our personality. Our character. See this figure holding out his hand in welcome? That is his Ka. The life force. The part of us that is immortal. The two parts of a human—his personality, his life force separated at death. The Ba would meet the Ka on the other side of the underworld. And be reunited for eternity. I was entranced."[9] Ancient rhythms permeate the modern world, as in *Four Baboons Adoring the Sun*. What is next reported is that B entombed a group of fellow tourists, killing them all and getting away with the crime. The confession in this special environment leads the two characters to an understanding and possible resolution that transcends judicial resolve.

Guare's literary roots showed themselves again in 2015 with productions of *More Stars Than There Are in Heaven* and *You Lied to Me about Centralia,* adaptations of two Tennessee Williams short stories. *More Stars Than There Are in Heaven* was given a staged reading 17 September at the Playhouse Creatures Theatre Company, New York City, in association with the Tennessee Williams Festival. It is an adaptation of "The Mattress by the Tomato Patch," based on Williams's experiences as a young, struggling writer employed by MGM and his interactions with his Marxist landlady. *You Lied to Me about Centralia* was produced 2 September by the Acting Company as one of six short plays on Williams collectively titled *Desire*. The event also included works by Beth Henley, Marcus Gardley, Rebecca Gilman, David Grimm, and Elizabeth Egloff. *You Lied to Me about Centralia* is based on a 1948 Williams story titled "Portrait of a Girl in Glass," featuring a young man named Jim looking back on a dinner party thrown by a friend. Jim turns out to be the gentleman caller from *The Glass Menagerie,* and he gives his account of his evening with the Wingfields.

This wide variety of short pieces is far from a minor part of Guare's career. Many of them, notably, are monologues and static dialogues. Effective on the stage, these pieces recall that Guare was an English major as a youth, as much enthralled by the power of the word as by the power of theatrical metaphors and dramatic action. His keen appreciation for the English language and his persistent effort to develop his craft as writer has resulted in a significant body of literary pieces for the theater, to which he is still adding.

Conclusion

Still active and engaged as a playwright and teacher and working actively throughout the American theater community in the capacity of elder statesman, John Guare has given much to the theater since the heady 1960s. There are few playwrights whose careers productively span six decades, and even fewer who have remained connected with the theater into their seventies. But Guare, ever the socially engaged activist, ever the man who thrives on human interconnection, continues to challenge the theater world with new works and to support it with numerous behind-the-scenes efforts to help maintain its cultural footing. He has worked diligently to expand the possibilities of the American theatrical form while training some of the brightest future playwriting stars.

Perhaps only Edward Albee rivals Guare among their contemporaries for sustained longevity and relevance throughout a fifty-plus-year career. In nearly every decade, Guare has made major theatrical contributions: *Muzeeka* (1967), *The House of Blue Leaves* (1971), *Marco Polo Sings a Solo* (1973), *Lydie Breeze* (1982), *Six Degrees of Separation* (1990), *Four Baboons Adoring the Sun* (1992), *A Free Man of Color* (2010). In each of these plays, he has refused to settle into comfortable formulas. Some have suggested that this refusal has cost him the popular—and sometimes critical—recognition that he deserves. Guare does not translate well into an adjective like "Beckettian" or "Shavian": his plays rarely exhibit easily identifiable earmarks like plays by others do.

Guare continues to play with theater with the same delight and enthusiasm he exhibited at the early stages of his career, ignoring critical exhortations to play the game by following the rules. Consider two of his most recent works, *A Free Man of Color* and *Funiage.* All three are full-scale, highly theatrical products indulging whimsy with the joy of a man still delighted by theater's potential, its ability to remain new to him and his audience. Ben Brantley, reviewing

A Free Man of Color, observed that "eclecticism has always been essential to Mr. Guare's writing, which at its best juggles mismatched elements of culture, high and low, with daring and dizzying skill. This is the man who memorably combined tabloid prurience (and famous-name dropping) with classic poetic lyricism in 'Landscape of the Body,' 'The House of Blue Leaves' and 'Six Degrees of Separation.'"[1]

Brantley went on to criticize the play for its lack of cohesion even as he acknowledged the high theatrical mash-up quality of Guare's previous works. David Rooney offered another criticism of *A Free Man of Color* that has recurred in reviews of Guare's other works: "At a time when the economic realities of commercial and nonprofit theater dictate that playwrights think small, the chutzpah of 'A Free Man of Color' commands respect. But in this rambunctious historical epic about race, class and the scars of nation-building—which ricochets among 40-plus characters in the U.S., France, Spain and colonial Haiti—John Guare demands too much of his audience."[2] Demanding too much of his audience may be something Guare does, but it may also be that he demands too much of an entrenched critical community that expects a comforting familiarity that he is just not prepared to offer.

Martin Denton called *Funiage* "antic and surreal" but noted that it jars against the evening's two preceding pieces, which "contain morsels of wisdom that remind us we're in the presence of one of America's playwriting titans."[3] The antic disposition of *Funiage* may or may not have succeeded in *3 Kinds of Exile,* but there is little doubt that Guare remains willing to experiment with audience expectations and theater's potential despite having reached a point where he could rightly rest on his laurels.

Critiqued throughout his career for his ambitious, often unwieldy projects and hard-to-label style, Guare continues to expand horizons rather than settle into a latter-day period of reassessment and reconstruction. He refuses to be tutored by the critics and willingly takes his lumps as he marches forward to the beat of his own drum, with the possible result being that the writers who follow in him will be better received by an establishment no longer looking only for the conventional and comfortable.

During a 2015 revival of *His Girl Friday,* Guare's 2003 adaptation of the Howard Hawks film of the same title, which was itself an adaptation of Ben Hecht and Charles Macarthur's play *The Front Page,* the playwright continued his career-long argument with the critics. About the production history of the play, he told an interviewer: "I did my homework, reading a dozen reviews of the play over the past decade and the critiques end up spending most of their time on how it doesn't measure up to the film, or quibbling about changes that they disapprove of. It gets tiresome. And while too many critics seem obsessed with examining the roots, sometimes they forget the point of a play is to entertain, to enjoy the bounty those roots produce. Oddly enough, for all the analysis, not one critic has said this play does not delight audiences, who seem to have loved each and every production so far."[4] Making theater work means entertaining an audience. Though still haunted by frequent critical misunderstanding, Guare has stood his ground.

Active to this day, Guare's theater agenda remains full of short plays as well as full-length undertakings. His work takes him from Broadway to regional nonprofits, helping a new generation of artists (playwrights as well as others) find their way in a profession full of challenges but full of rewards. In 2012 he received the Greenfield Prize, sponsored by the Heritage Retreat in Sarasota, Florida, commissioning him to write a new play. In late 2015 Guare reported, "I am deep in that play as we speak."[5] Clearly not of a retiring inclination, John Guare continues to contribute to American theater.

NOTES

Chapter 1—Understanding John Guare

1. Plunka, *Black Comedy of John Guare,* 11.
2. Guare, "War against the Kitchen Sink," vii.
3. Qtd. in Cattaneo, "John Guare," 87.
4. Guare, introduction to *The House of Blue Leaves,* 7.
5. Guare, "War against the Kitchen Sink," xii.
6. Hall, preface, ix–x.
7. Hessel and Lichtenberg, "Guare and Company," 4.
8. Vanden Heuvel, "From Paradise to Parasite," 234.
9. See especially Esslin, *Theatre of the Absurd.*

Chapter 2—Early Work

1. Guare, *Loveliest Afternoon of the Year,* 94.
2. LeSueur, "Two Plays by John Guare."
3. Plunka, *Black Comedy of John Guare,* 52.
4. Guare, *Muzeeka,* 6.
5. Curry, *John Guare,* 80.
6. Bunce, "'Muzeeka,' 'Red Cross,' 'Statue'"; Hummler, "*Red Cross* and *Muzeeka,*" 72.
7. Tallmer, "Across the Footlights," 22.
8. Oliver, "Off Broadway: Mr. Lowell and Mr. Haigh."
9. Qtd. in Bosworth, "Yes for a Young Man's Fantasies."
10. Guare, *Home Fires,* 26.
11. Barnes, "Theater: Guare's Humorous 'Cop-Out.'"
12. Guare, *Kissing Sweet,* 11.

Chapter 3—*The House of Blue Leaves* (1971) and *Two Gentlemen of Verona* (1971)

1. Guare, *House of Blue Leaves,* 5.
2. DiGaetani, "John Guare," 109.
3. Plunka, *Black Comedy of John Guare,* 233.
4. Novick, "Very Funny."
5. Hewes, "Under the Rainbow," 10.
6. Gussow, "Revisiting a Realm of Broken Dreams."
7. Brantley, "Papal Visit Has Dreamers Dreaming."
8. Hessel and Lichtenberg, "Guare and Company," 5.
9. Guare, introduction to *Two Gentlemen of Verona,* 6.

Chapter 4—After *Blue Leaves*

1. Guare, *Marco Polo Sings a Solo*, 4.
2. Marks, "'Marco Polo Sings a Solo.'"
3. Guare, *Rich and Famous*, 6.
4. Guare, *Landscape of the Body*, 148.
5. Guare, *In Fireworks Lie Secret Codes*, 13.
6. Brantley, "Gold Lamé Dreams."
7. Guare, *Bosoms and Neglect*, 217.
8. Gussow, "Stage: John Guare's 'Bosom and Neglect.'"
9. Guare, *In Fireworks Lie Secret Codes*, 13.

Chapter 5—*Atlantic City* (1980)

1. Canby, review of *Atlantic City*.

Chapter 6—Capturing America's Heritage

1. Qtd. in Hinson, "Ordinary Absurdity."
2. Guare, introduction to *Lydie Breeze*, 8.
3. Andreach, *John Guare's Theatre*, 99.
4. Qtd. in Berkvist, "John Guare Stirs Up a *Breeze*."
5. Guare, *Lydie Breeze*, 19.
6. Guare, *Women and Water*, 5.
7. Rich, "Stage Guare's 'Lydie Breeze.'"
8. Brantley, "Theater Review; Bewildered Ringmaster."
9. Guare, "Author's Note," in *Few Stout Individuals*, 4.

Chapter 7—*Six Degrees of Separation* (1990)

1. Guare, *Six Degrees of Separation*, 81.
2. Vanden Heuvel, "From Paradise to Parasite," 234.
3. "Judge Tells Con Man to Avoid Playwright."
4. Plunka, *Black Comedy of John Guare*, 189–90.

Chapter 8—*Four Baboons Adoring the Sun* (1992)

1. Hall, preface, x.
2. Guare, *Four Baboons Adoring the Sun*, 4.
3. Drake, "Crashing Symbols."

Chapter 9—*A Free Man of Color* (2010)

1. Brantley, "Gaudy Swashbuckle through History."
2. Healy, "Guare's Gamble of Epic Proportions."
3. Guare, *Free Man of Color*, 5.
4. Mansbridge, "Racing toward History," 414.
5. Isherwood, "Swimming in a Sea of Stories."

Chapter 10—A Career of Short Works

1. Isherwood, "Swimming in a Sea of Stories."
2. John, Guare, *Talking Dog*, 137.
3. Guare, *Greenwich Mean*, 27, 28.

4. Van Gelder, "Take It Easy, Ophelia."
5. Guare, *Woman at a Threshold, Beckoning*, 24.
6. Guare, *What It Was Like,* 347.
7. Soloski, "John Guare Looks to the East."
8. Red Bull Theater website, www.redbulltheater.com/#!about/c1q46.
9. Guare, *Between,* 102.

Conclusion

1. Brantley, "Gaudy Swashbuckle through History."
2. Rooney, "'Free Man of Color.'"
3. Denton, review of *3 Kinds of Exile.*
4. Murray, "Playwright John Guare talks about 'His Girl Friday.'"
5. Personal correspondence, 2 September 2015.

SELECTED BIBLIOGRAPHY

Works by John Guare

PLAYS

Between. In *The Best American Short Plays, 2013–2014,* edited by William W. Demastes, 93–105. New York: Applause Theatre and Cinema Books, 2015.

Blue Monologue. In *The Best American Short Plays, 2007–2008,* edited by Barbara Parisi, 374–77. New York: Applause Theatre and Cinema Books, 2009.

Bosoms and Neglect. In *"The House of Blue Leaves" and Two Other Plays,* 169–254. New York: Plume, 1987.

Chaucer in Rome. New York: Dramatists Play Service, 2002.

A Day for Surprises. In *"Four Baboons Adoring the Sun" and Other Plays,* 103–12. New York: Vintage, 1993.

Elzbieta Erased. In *The Best American Short Plays, 2011–2012,* edited by William W. Demastes, 13–43. New York: Applause Theatre and Cinema Books, 2013.

A Few Stout Individuals. New York: Dramatists Play Service, 2003.

Four Baboons Adoring the Sun. In *"Four Baboons Adoring the Sun" and Other Plays,* 1–71. New York: Vintage, 1993.

Gardenia. New York: Dramatists Play Circle, 1982.

The General of Hot Desire. In *"The General of Hot Desire" and Other Plays,* 7–22. New York: Dramatists Play Service, 1999.

Greenwich Mean. In *"The General of Hot Desire" and Other Plays,* 25–30. New York: Dramatists Play Service, 1999.

Home Fires. In *The War against the Kitchen Sink*. Vol. 1 of *The Collected Works of John Guare,* 23–44. Lyme, N.H.: Smith & Kraus, 1996.

The House of Blue Leaves. In *"The House of Blue Leaves" and Two Other Plays,* 1–87. New York: Plume, 1987.

In Fireworks Lie Secret Codes. New York: Dramatists Play Service, 1981. Also in *"Four Baboons Adoring the Sun" and Other Plays,* 143–60. New York: Vintage, 1993.

Kissing Sweet. In *"Kissing Sweet" and "A Day for Surprises,"* 4–13. New York: Dramatists Play Service, 1971.

Lake Hollywood. New York: Dramatists Play Service, 2000.

The Landscape of the Body. In *"The House of Blue Leaves" and Two Other Plays,* 89–167. New York: Plume, 1987.

The Loveliest Afternoon of the Year. In *"Four Baboons Adoring the Sun" and Other Plays,* 91–102. New York: Vintage, 1993.

Lydie Breeze (Part I: Bulfinch's Mythology; Part II: The Sacredness of the Next Task). Woodstock, N.Y.: Overlook, 1982.

Marco Polo Sings a Solo. New York: Dramatists Play Service, 1977.

Moon under Miami. In *The War against the Kitchen Sink*. Vol. 1 of *The Collected Works of John Guare*, 93–149. Lyme, N.H.: Smith & Kraus, 1996. Also in *"The General of Hot Desire" and Other Plays*, 45–69. New York: Dramatists Play Service, 1999.

Muzeeka. New York: Dramatists Play Service, 1968. Also in *"Four Baboons Adoring the Sun" and Other Plays*, 113–42. New York: Vintage, 1993.

New York Actor. In *"Four Baboons Adoring the Sun" and Other Plays*, 175–88. New York: Vintage, 1993.

Rich and Famous. New York: Dramatists Play Service, 1977.

Six Degrees of Separation. New York: Random House, 1990.

Something I'll Tell You Tuesday. In *"Four Baboons Adoring the Sun" and Other Plays*, 73–89. New York: Vintage, 1993.

The Talking Dog. In *"Four Baboons Adoring the Sun" and Other Plays*, 161–74. New York: Vintage, 1993. Rpt. in *Orchards: Plays Inspired by the Short Stories of Anton Chekhov*, 125–39. New York: Knopf, 1986. Rpt. again in *"The General of Hot Desire" and Other Plays*, 31–41. New York: Dramatists Play Service, 1999.

Two Gentlemen of Verona, Adapted by Mel Shapiro and John Guare. New York: Holt, Rinehart & Winston, 1973.

What It Was Like. In *The Best American Short Plays, 2009–2010*, edited by Barbara Parisi, 342–47. New York: Applause Theatre and Cinema Books, 2011.

Woman at a Threshold, Beckoning. In *The Best American Short Plays, 2003–2004*, edited by Glenn Young, 1–28. New York: Applause Theatre and Cinema Books, 2006.

Women and Water. New York: Dramatists Play Service, 1990.

FILM SCRIPTS

Atlantic City. In *Scenario: The Magazine of Screenwriting Art* 2, no. 2 (1996): 154–84.

Taking Off. By Milos Foreman, John Guare, Jean-Claude Carrière, and John Klein. New York: New American Library, 1971.

SELECTED ESSAYS

"Author's Note." In *A Few Stout Individuals*, 4–8. New York: Dramatists Play Service, 2003.

Introduction to *The Collected Short Plays of Thornton Wilder*. Vol. 1. Edited by Donald Gallup and Tappan Wilder. New York: Theatre Communications Group, 1997.

"Author's Notes." In *Women and Water*, 3–7. New York: Dramatists Play Service, 1990.

Chuck Close: A Life 1988–1995. New York: Thames and Hudson, 1995.

"Foreword: All the Things You Are." In *The Best American Short Plays, 2007–2008*, edited by Barbara Parisi, ix–xiii. New York: Applause Theatre and Cinema Books, 2009.

Introduction to *Lydie Breeze*, 7–13. Woodstock, N.Y.: Overlook, 1982.

"Introduction to *"The House of Blue Leaves" and Other Plays*, 3–8. New York: Plume, 1987.

Preface in *"The House of Blue Leaves" and Other Plays*, vii–xiii. New York: Plume, 1987.

"Production Note." In *Six Degrees of Separation*, xi–xiii. New York: Random House, 1990.

"The War against the Kitchen Sink: A Preface." In *The War against the Kitchen Sink*, vi–xii. Vol. 1 of *The Collected Works of John Guare*. Lyme, N.H.: Smith & Kraus, 1996.

SELECTED INTERVIEWS

Bryer, Jackson. "John Guare." In *The Playwright's Art: Conversations with Contemporary American Dramatists,* 70–85. New Brunswick, N.J.: Rutgers University Press, 1995.

Cattaneo, Ann. "John Guare: The Art of Theater IX." *Paris Review* no. 125 (1992): 69–103.

———. "The Making of a Playwright and His Plays." *Dramatists Guild Quarterly* (Winter 1992): 6–14.

DiGaetani, John. "John Guare." In *A Search for a Postmodern Theater: Interviews with Contemporary Playwrights,* edited by John DiGaetani, 105–11. Westport, Conn.: Greenwood, 1991.

Martin, Nicholas. "Chaos and Other Muses." *American Theatre* April 1999, 26–29, 52.

Murray, Larry. "Playwright John Guare Talks about 'His Girl Friday,' from Stage to Film to Stage Again." Berkshire on Stage and Screen, 17 July 2015, http://berkshireonstage.com/2015/07/17/playwright-john-guare-here-to-work-on-his-girl-friday-laugh-a-minute-comedy-at-barrington-stage/.

Savran, David. "John Guare." In *In Their Own Words: Contemporary American Playwrights,* edited by David Savran, 84–99. New York: Theatre Communications Group, 1988.

Works about John Guare and Secondary Materials

Andreach, Robert J. *Creating the Self in the Contemporary American Theatre.* Carbondale: Southern Illinois University Press, 1998.

———. "Ibsen's *A Doll's House* Reimagined in Guare's *Marco Polo Sings a Solo.*" *Journal of Dramatic Theory and Criticism* 21, no. 2 (2007): 49–63.

———. *John Guare's Theatre: The Art of Connecting.* Newcastle upon Tyne: Cambridge Scholars, 2009.

Barnes, Clive. "Theater: Guare's Humorous 'Cop-Out.'" *New York Times* 8 April 1969.

Berkvist, Robert. "John Guare Stirs Up a *Breeze.*" *New York Times* 21 February 1982.

Bernstein, Samuel J. *The Strands Entwined: A New Direction in American Drama.* Boston: Northeastern University Press, 1980.

Bigsby, Christopher. *Contemporary American Playwrights.* Cambridge: Cambridge University Press, 1999.

Billington, Michael. Rev. of *Six Degrees of Separation. Guardian* 19 January 2010.

Bosworth, Patricia. "Yes for a Young Man's Fantasies." *New York Times* 7 March 1971.

Brantley, Ben. "A Gaudy Swashbuckle through History." *New York Times* 18 November 2010.

———. "Gold Lamé Dreams Dashed by Polyester Reality in 'Landscape of the Body.'" *New York Times* 17 April 2006.

———. "A Papal Visit Has Dreamers Dreaming." *New York Times* 25 April 2011.

———. "Theater Review; Bewildered Ringmaster in a Celebrity Circus." *New York Times* 13 May 2002.

Bunce, Alan N. "'Muzeeka,' 'Red Cross,' 'Statue.' New Faces." *Christian Science Monitor* 10 May 1968.

Canby, Vincent. Rev. of *Atlantic City. New York Times* 3 April 1981.

Carroll, Dennis. "Not-Quite Mainstream Male Playwrights: Guare, Durang, and Rabe." In *Contemporary American Theatre,* edited by Bruce King, 41–61. New York: St. Martin's.

Chin, Daryl. "From Popular to Pop: The Arts in/of Commerce." *Performing Arts Journal* 37 (1991): 5–20.

Clum, John M. *Acting Gay: Male Homosexuality in Modern Drama.* New York: Columbia University Press, 1992.

Cohn, Ruby. "Camp Cruelty, Colloquialism." In *Comic Relief: Humour in Contemporary American Literature,* edited by Sarah Blacher Cohen, 281–303. Urbana: University of Illinois Press.

Comer, Brooke, "*Six Degrees of Separation:* Bringing Chaos under Control." *American Cinematographer* (March 1994): 50–54.

Cohn, Ruby. *New American Dramatists, 1960–1980.* New York: Grove.

Curry, Jane Kathleen. *John Guare: A Research and Production Sourcebook.* Westport, Conn.: Greenwood, 2002.

Denton, Martin. Rev. of *3 Kinds of Exile.* nytheatre.com 12 June 2013, http://nytheatre.com/Review/martin-denton-2013-6-12-3-kinds-of-exile.

Drake, Sylvie. "Crashing Symbols: Guare's Play Juggles Metaphors, Drops a Few." *Los Angeles Times* 19 March 1992.

Gillian, Jennifer. "Staging a Stages Crisis in Masculinity: Race and Masculinity in *Six Degrees of Separation.*" *American Drama* 9, no. 2 (2000): 50–73.

Goetz, Ruth, "John Guare." *Dramatics* May 1983, 4–6, 28–30.

Greene, Alexis. "The New Comedy of Manners." *Theater* 23 (1992): 79–83.

Gross, Robert F. "Life in a Silken Net: Mourning the Beloved Monstrous in *Lydie Breeze.*" *Journal of Dramatic Theory and Criticism* 9, no. 1 (1994): 21–42.

Gussow, Mel. "Revisiting a Realm of Broken Dreams." *New York Times* 6 April 1986.

———. "Stage: John Guare's 'Bosom and Neglect.'" *New York Times* 13 April 1986.

Hall, Sir Peter. Preface to *"Four Baboons Adoring the Sun" and Other Plays,* ix–xii. New York: Vintage, 1993.

Harrop, John. "'Ibsen Translated by Lewis Carroll': The Theatre of John Guare." *New Theatre Quarterly* 3, no. 10 (1987): 150–54.

———. "NTQ Checklist No. 3: John Guare." *New Theatre Quarterly* 3, no. 10 (1987): 160–77.

Healy, Patrick, "Guare's Gamble of Epic Proportions." *New York Times* 10 November 2010.

Hessel, Hannah, and Drew Lichtenberg. "Guare & Company." *Asides: A Publication of the Shakespeare Theatre Company* no. 3 (2011–12): 4–6.

Hewes, Henry. "The Playwright as Voyager." *Saturday Review World* 20 November 1973, 48.

———. "Under the Rainbow." *Saturday Review* 20 March 1971, 10.

Hinson, Hal. "Ordinary Absurdity." *Washington Post* 17 June 1984.

Holmberg, Arthur. "Waning of Spirituality Perplexes Artists Today." *American Theatre,* June 1991, 44–46.

Hummler, Richard. "*Red Cross* and *Muzeeka.*" *Variety* 1 May 1968, 72.

Isherwood, Charles. "Swimming in a Sea of Stories: 'Are You There, McPhee?' by John Guare, at Berlind Theater." *New York Times* 15 May 2012.

"Judge Tells Con Man to Avoid Playwright." *New York Times* 7 May 1991.

Lahr, John. "The Guare Essentials." *Vogue,* June 1992, 144–45, 178.

———. *Up against the Fourth Wall: Essays in Modern Theater.* New York: Grove, 1970.

Mansbridge, Joanna. "Racing toward History: Utopia and Progress in John Guare's *A Free Man of Color.*" *Modern Drama* 58, no. 4 (2015): 413–36.

Marks, Peter. "'Marco Polo Sings a Solo': Alienation on an Iceberg." *New York Times* 28 September 1998.

Marranca, Bonnie, and Gautam Dasgupta. "John Guare." In *American Playwrights: A Critical Survey,* 41–52. New York: Drama Book Specialists, 1981.

Novick, Julius. "Very Funny—or a Long Sick Joke." *New York Times* 21 February 1971.

"N.Y. Judge Dismisses Con Artist's Suit over 'Six Degrees.'" *Entertainment Litigation Reporter* 8 June 1992.

Oliver, Edith. "Off Broadway: Mr. Lowell and Mr. Haigh." *New Yorker* 11 May 1968, 86–92.

Orr, John. "Paranoia and Celebrity in American Dramatic Writing, 1970–1990." In *The Theatrical Gamut: Notes for a Post-Brechtian Stage,* edited by Enoch Brater, 141–58. Ann Arbor: University of Michigan Press, 1995.

Plunka, Gene A. *The Black Comedy of John Guare.* Newark: University of Delaware Press, 2002.

———. "The Black Comedy of Urban Neurosis: John Guare's *The House of Blue Leaves.*" *Studies in the Humanities* 25 (1998): 38–52.

———. "Freud and the Psychology of Neurosis: John Guare's *Bosoms and Neglect.*" *Papers on Language and Literature* 36 (2000): 93–108.

———. "Guare's *Four Baboons Adoring the Sun.*" *Explicator* (2000): 116–18.

Rich, Frank. "Stage Guare's 'Lydie Breeze.'" *New York Times* 28 February 1982.

Rooney, David. "'A Free Man of Color'—Theater Review." *Hollywood Reporter* 18 November 2010.

Rose, Lloyd. "A New American Master." *Atlantic Monthly* March 1984, 120–24.

"'Six Degrees of Separation' Civil Rights and Invasion of Privacy Dismissal Affirmed by New York Appellate Court." *Entertainment Law Reporter* 15, no. 6 (1993).

Sleuthaus, Gordon E. "Chaotics and Many Degrees of Separation in John Guare's *Six Degree of Separation.*" *American Drama* 11, no. 1 (2002): 73–93.

Soloski, Alexis. "John Guare Looks to the East in *3 Kinds of Exile.*" *Village Voice* 12 June 2013.

Steinberg, Jacques. "Jury Acquits Man of One Count in the Harassment of Playwright." *New York Times* 2 October 1992.

Stuart, Jan. "Stars & Strife Forever." *American Theatre* April 1985, 12–18.

Tallmer, Jerry. "Across the Footlights: America Hoo-Hoo." *New York Post* 29 April 1968.

Turina, Ana Fernandez-Caparros. "The Geography of Imagination: Urban Mapping of Social Networks in John Guare's *Six Degrees of Separation.*" *South Atlantic Review* 76, no. 4 (2011): 57–75.

Vanden Heuvel, Mike. "From Paradise to Parasite: Information Theory, Noise, and Disequilibrium in John Guare's *Six Degrees of Separation.*" In *Interrogating America through Performance and Theatre,* edited by William W. Demastes and Iris Smith Fischer, 233–42. New York: Palgrave Macmillan, 2007.

Van Gelder, Lawrence. "Take It Easy, Ophelia; A Swim Will Do You Good." *New York Times* 9 June 2003.

Wilmeth, Don B. "John Guare." In *American Playwrights since 1945: A Guide to Scholarship, Criticism, and Performance,* edited by Philip Kolin, 142–54. Westport, Conn.: Greenwood, 1989.

Wolfe, Graham. "'Doorways' and 'Blank Spaces': Intertextual Connection in John Guare's *Six Degrees of Separation.*" In *Intertextuality in American Drama: Critical*

Essays on Eugene O'Neill, Susan Glaspell, Thornton Wilder, Arthur Miller, and Other Playwrights, edited by Drew Eisenhauer and Brenda Murphy, 217–31. Jefferson, N.C.: McFarland, 2013.

Zimmerman, David. "Six Degrees of Distinction: Connection, Contagion, and the Aesthetics of Anything." *Arizona Quarterly* 35, no. 3 (1999): 106–33.

INDEX